A/E/C
MARKETING
FUNDAMENTALS
Your Keys to Success

A/E/C MARKETING FUNDAMENTALS
Your Keys to Success

by Holly R. Bolton, Julie Huval,
Stephen A. Jones, Kevin Miller,
David M. Shelton, and Ronald D. Worth

Edited by Richard A. Belle

SMPS
PUBLICATIONS

www.smps.org

PUBLICATIONS

First published in 2004 by BNI Publications, Inc.

SMPS PUBLICATIONS is an imprint of the Society for Marketing Professional Services (SMPS)
123 N. Pitt Street, Suite 400, Alexandria, VA 22314
800.292.7677 | 703.549.6117 | www.smps.org

SMPS is a not-for-profit, professional organization established to promote research and education that advances the body of knowledge in the field of professional services marketing and develops a greater understanding of the role and value of marketing in the A/E/C industry.

Cover Photo: RADY School of Management at UC San Diego. Copyright © 2008 by Paul Turang
Cover Design: J.H. Flores
Chapter headings and back cover photography: Paul Turang and Sam Kittner (see *Credits*, p.162).
Book design and layout: Gabrielle David / www.gabrielle-david.com

Library of Congress Control Number: 2015932957

ISBN-13: 978-0-9769284-0-9 (Paperback)
ISBN-13: 978-0-9769284-2-3 (eBook)

10   9   8   7   6   5   4   3   2   1

Published in the United States of America

Second Edition | First Printing

SMPS BOOKS are available for sale on most online retailers in the U.S., U.K., Canada and Australia. Books are also available to the trade through Ingram and Amazon.com. For more information, contact info@smps.org.

TABLE OF CONTENTS

CHAPTER THREE
ALTERNATIVE PROJECT DELIVERY: MEETING THE OWNER'S PROJECT DEMANDS ■ 43

CHAPTER FOUR
MARKET RESEARCH: KNOW YOURSELF, YOUR CLIENT, YOUR COMPETITORS ■ 61

CHAPTER FIVE
DEVELOP YOUR MARKETING STRATEGY ■ 77

CHAPTER SIX
CREATING YOUR MARKETING COMMUNICATIONS PLAN ■ 97

CHAPTER SEVEN
IMPLEMENTING YOUR MARKETING STRATEGY: TACTICS AND TOOLS ■ 117

List of Figures and Examples

INTRODUCTION

FOR MANY BUSINESS PEOPLE, marketing means selling at a large scale, but in actuality, marketing is the art and science of delivering value and creating awareness to existing and potential customers. Unfortunately, while marketing is a critical component of every business, it is one of the least understood and underutilized components, particularly within the architecture, engineering and construction (A/E/C) industry. This is because the industry is unique: the sales cycle is long, the buyers are diverse and price tags are large, which is why A/E/C firms do not fit the traditional marketing model.

Marketing is not second nature to most people. We would like to think that the quality of our work is easily perceived and stands on its own. Assuming that excellence finds its own reward, many of us feel it is unseemly to promote our work, but the world does not work this way. For decades, professional service firms have relied on reputation, relationships and repeat business to drive business growth, with marketing viewed as a way to support these business development efforts, but rarely a major driver. Now, times are changing. In today's hyper-competitive marketplace, and particularly in the design and construction industry, the need for an effective and robust marketing strategy is more compelling than it has ever been. Marketing plays a vital role in business because it can help your firm reach potential customers, and convert that awareness into paying clients. Without marketing, potential customers may not be aware of the services your business has to offer. Without customers, your business may meet its demise. Here is how *A/E/C Marketing Fundamentals* can help.

A/E/C Marketing Fundamentals is a direct realization of the Society for Marketing Professional Services (SMPS), and its new imprint, SMPS Publications. When *A/E/C Marketing Fundamentals* first published in 2004, the goal was to provide marketers with the resources and ideas necessary to adapt to the numerous standards changing in the A/E/C industry. This second edition goes even further. Besides bringing marketers up-to-speed on the latest resources and project delivery methods, it provides creative, up-to-date compelling examples of marketing material – electronic, online and print – illustrating best practices in strategy, design and content by A/E/C firms. So whether you are new to the A/E/C community and working on your very first job, a more seasoned professional who is taking on marketing responsibilities for the first time, or an experienced marketer, *A/E/C Marketing Fundamentals* can help you learn some new core principles and effective strategies to improve your job performance, as well as gain new business for your firm.

Every generation probably feels that it is confronting unprecedented and unique challenges. On a superficial level, this is certainly true; yet one of the key themes, and probably the most important argument you will encounter in this volume, is that the "rules of the game" for our industry have changed more in the last decade than in any comparable period. The market expectations are hugely different, and if you fail to grasp the significance of these changes, and insist on treating your clients and competitors in the same manner that you would have just a few years ago, you will be left behind.

There was a time when we were disciplinarians in our own fields, but nowadays, firms no longer have the luxury of having a "hard" technical staff and a "soft" marketing staff because clients have demands and higher expectations. A/E/C firms are becoming increasingly market-driven, and if a business is to remain innovative, then marketing is the job of every employee. Aggressive designers and contractors are taking the necessary steps to involve all of their personnel in marketing. Superintendents are being trained to network with subcontractors on site for other project opportunities. Project managers are becoming experts in continuing relationships with existing clients. Even the accounting staff is beginning to recognize the importance of servicing customers to ensure a steady flow of repeat business. Although the idea of a market-driven culture in the design and construction industry was almost unheard of a few years ago, today there is a critical need to instill this culture within each member of the team, particularly any member who interacts with clients on a regular basis. Progressive A/E/C firms of all types have already begun to enhance their business culture to reflect these dynamics so they can succeed in this new, competitive environment.

Certainly, a wave of new technologies is being used to reach and research existing and prospective customers. Even tools thought of as "new" a decade ago, such as Internet advertising, emails, text messaging, and social media are now seen as the norm or in some cases, even antiquated. Newer technologies, such as GPS and smart phone applications, are becoming increasingly important. Two major tools being used today are customer relationship management systems (CRMs) and building information modeling (BIM). Yet many in the A/E/C industry think that online marketing consists of a website and Facebook account, when nothing could be further from the truth. In fact, the A/E/C industry has been one of the slowest to embrace inbound marketing as a tool than other professional service providers.

Without trivializing the role of technology and its importance, the key to successful marketing remains the same: It is imperative for you to have a solid strategy in place that will help potential customers decide whether or not to choose you initially or for repeat business. Once you have developed your strategy, your next step is to work closely with your technical staff, which is more often than not an untapped business development tool. Actively engage them in your business development efforts by educating them in the firm's strategies, goals, history, and capabilities. Encourage them to offer additional services to current clients and seek new commissions through their personal and professional networks of contacts. Bear in mind that in order to collect quality leads utilizing the latest technology requires time, energy and money to ensure active and consistent results. That is why it is so important to support your team's interests in professional organizations, and seek their input when analyzing potential opportunities. Think of it this way: If business is all about people and money, and the art of persuading one to part from the other, then marketing is all about having the right team in place to help you find paying clients.

Today we are presented with a wealth of new opportunities and resources that can lead companies toward favorable results. Clearly, marketing is not what it used to be, and it is the intention of *A/E/C Marketing Fundamentals* to introduce marketers to new realities that can enhance successful marketing practices that have been standard for most of us for a very long time. Some of the topics may be new to you, while others may serve to reinforce approaches that you have already developed. Chapters 1, 2, and 3 describe the new fast-paced, high-expectation environment that is strikingly different from the marketing world of just a few years ago. Chapters 4, 5, 6 and 7 present strategies you should adopt to become a successful marketer.

These chapters stand up on their own; however, there is a benefit to reading them in consecutive order because each one builds on concepts introduced from a previous chapter. To help you plot your reading path, each chapter begins with a short bulleted summary, "Things You Will Learn from This Chapter," which prompts you to keep in mind these objectives as you follow the narrative. At the end of each chapter, we also provide "Things to Think About," a select group of self-assessment questions that serve as a reinforcement of the broader implications of what you have just read. Each of the seven chapters in this volume focuses on issues that can help you become a better marketer, but our discussion is not exhaustive. We have also included an "Annotated Bibliography" that contains a list of books and other resources we used to write this volume. Following up on these resources will help you explore some of the issues we have raised in greater depth. As the technology supporting the A/E/C community evolves and advances, so does the terminology for the industry. To help understand the terms used in this volume, as well as better communicate among the members of this community, we offer a "Glossary" of A/E/C terms.

Many A/E/C firms have become so focused on RFPs, proposals and interviews that their marketing efforts have taken a back seat. Some firms believe that online marketing is not for their business, or that their business is "different." Although larger firms have begun to utilize A/E/C marketing strategies, this is not the case among mid- to smaller-sized firms. This lag has created a massive opportunity for early adopters of digital marketing to leap ahead of their rivals while this rare window of opportunity remains open. That is why SMPS decided to issue a second edition of *A/E/C Marketing Fundamentals,* so that it can help service professionals in the industry learn about, and take advantage of emerging technologies, global competition, new partnerships and project deliveries, and the evolution of online and digital marketing.

The strategies and real world experiences contained in this volume were brought together by experts, who have given serious thought on how to create and implement a viable marketing strategy. I would like to take this opportunity to acknowledge the time and efforts of our contributors in the reissuance of *A/E/C Marketing Fundamentals.* Without their collective efforts, this volume would not be possible.

Everything you read from here on has only one purpose: To help you secure a more profitable business relationship with your customers. It is my hope that with the right focus and approach, *A/E/C Marketing Fundamentals* can help you refine and improve your marketing strategy, and position your firm for greater success. ■

– Richard R. Belle, IOM, CAE
President of Belle Communications, LLC

CHAPTER ONE

New Realities for A/E/C Marketers

Things You Will Learn From This Chapter

- How marketing strategies are changing as a result of the virtual project

- New collaborative opportunities for designers, engineers, contractors, and owners

- How to assess risk appropriately

- Key principles for developing and sustaining customer relationships

YOUR WORLD HAS CHANGED. This may sound like a banal truism, but if you do not understand exactly how the architecture, engineering and construction (A/E/C) industry landscape has evolved, you will not be able to support your firm effectively.

Today, marketing professionals are enjoying opportunities that were unheard of just a few years ago. Yet, despite the evolution of online marketing, and the advent of new technologies that are currently reshaping the landscape, many A/E/C firms have stubbornly held on to traditional marketing methods (print, trade shows, cold calling), including RFPs and proposals, which have begun to decrease in relevance.

What A/E/C firms fail to understand is that online marketing is an expansion of traditional marketing systems, and that it has the potential to drive significantly more growth and profitability while costing less on the bottom line. While an online marketing strategy requires time, energy and money to ensure active and consistent involvement, the rewards are immense: sophisticated media campaigns engage potential clients, which in turn creates brand loyalty.

This technological burst of activity has also encouraged new trends and strategic creativity, including an interactive environment that has revolutionized project delivery methods. This includes customer relationship management systems (CRMs), building information modeling (BIM), and computer-aided design (CAD), enabling more efficient virtual collaboration in cross-functional projects that can be accessed on a cloud. When you combine viral media campaigns and the latest project delivery methods, it encourages knowledge sharing and innovative processes on a global level. We are truly becoming a global village.

For you to succeed as an A/E/C marketer, it is essential that you understand just how much your world has changed and confront some challenges that were unimaginable until very recently. If you want to successfully market your A/E/C firm in the future, it is time to shift your marketing paradigm. In this chapter, we will introduce two new paradigms that have transformed the way A/E/C services are marketed.

The Double-Edged Sword for Marketers: The Virtual Project

The first is the advent of the virtual project. All your marketing strategies, from firm branding and capture strategies, to project implementation and client retention efforts, are now just as likely to take place digitally as they are in person. Traditional marketing elements such as letters, contracts, brochures, and qualifications statements are now sent electronically, and can be received instantly by potential clients. CDs and DVDs often replace brochures, while oral presentations have morphed into video conferencing. In fact, marketers can perform services today without ever having to meet their customer face-to-face, and it is not unusual for a sale to result without the customer ever having personally met with the designer or contractor.

Being instantaneously linked to both collaborators and clients can be a mixed blessing, because your competitors have the same access and, as a result, your clients have significantly higher expectations in terms of quality, cost, and schedule. What will that mean to your firm, both for generating business, and for project implementation and client retention?

The Shift from Outbound to Inbound Marketing Strategies

The marketing industry's focus has shifted from outbound marketing strategies to inbound marketing. Advances in technology have opened up new ways to communicate a firm's thought leadership with its audiences. Whereas outbound marketing consists of pushing a sales message out using tactics such as advertising, direct mail, and cold calling; inbound marketing, which helps clients find your firm based on their needs and your expertise, is delivered using platforms such as blogs, white papers, and presentations. While outbound marketing strategies can still be useful, inbound marketing strategies can help differentiate your firm from the plethora of other messages and information out there.

Time Compression

Today's consumers have become accustomed to instant gratification, from the music we download and the goods we purchase, to the food we consume. Products and services are now customized, and we expect them to be delivered immediately, if not sooner. Because manufacturers and service providers have to contend with this expectation in their own industries, they in turn expect the design and construction industry to respond the same way.

Although no building or facility can be completed instantly, clients are now demanding that designers and contractors greatly compress design and construction schedules so that they in turn can compete effectively in their own industries. A/E/C marketers must be aware of these expectations, and confidently present their company's qualifications and capabilities to meet each project's specific time requirements.

The Global Village

The ability to communicate directly from and with any destination has created a global village; for many architects and contractors, it has also created an opportunity for entry into distant markets. Although billions of dollars of domestic billings are derived from foreign projects, foreign firms have managed to capture billions of dollars' worth of domestic billings in the United States. This is just one example of how the A/E/C industry is growing into an international business that no longer relies on local business and talent; it has limitless boundaries. Firms in the United States are eagerly teaming, partnering, and forming strategic alliances around the world, so that they can compete more effectively. Besides hiring multilingual professionals to increase their domestic in-house capabilities, and to facilitate competition abroad, there is no longer a need to maintain a full-time staff beyond any given project. The world has truly become a global village, and the implications of this trend have penetrated well into the A/E/C industries, forever changing how it is marketed, sold, and completed.

Digital Capabilities

Computer hardware and software have revolutionized the way business is conducted in the A/E/C profession, as well as in the companies run by our industry's clients. Computer-aided design (CAD) has given way to 3D, 4D, and 5D modeling, not only greatly facilitating collaboration among project members, but also ensuring greater cost control and predictability for project tasks. Is your firm fully utilizing these tools? Equally importantly, as a marketer for your firm, how do you explain how these new skills and technologies benefit potential clients in a manner that successfully differentiates your firm's capabilities?

We're All Friends Now: New Opportunities for Collaboration

The second paradigm shift the industry has seen in recent years is the way designers, engineers, and contractors interact with each other, as well as with owners and clients, during the course of a project. The traditional model for design and construction, despite best intentions, frequently became adversarial; architects and contractors became involved at different phases of a project and had different relationships and understandings with the client. If, and when, problems developed over the course of a project (schedule delays, cost overruns, change-orders, etc.), each side tended to blame the other for the difficulties because they had different contractual assumptions and fiduciary commitments.

In recent years, there has been an explosion of new contractual relationships that appear to better facilitate collaboration. Termed alternative project delivery (APD), these new strategies allow and often encourage sharing of risk and responsibility. As a marketer, you need to understand how these new relationships will affect your approaches to client capture and retention, as well as your view of erstwhile competitors.

No Longer a Commodity Service?

Perhaps the biggest change to come out of APD strategies is the gradual "decommoditization" of design and construction services. Unfortunately, today's design and construction profession is frequently treated as a commodity service, with the lowest price being the key to a successful project. Spurred on by fierce competition and the need for clients to reduce operating costs and increase profits, commodity pricing has spread from department stores such as Walmart to the medical (HMOs), law, and construction industries. Clients often place too much emphasis on the fees charged by design and construction professionals, when in fact their costs, in comparison to the project's overall costs, are actually minuscule. The averages taken from a wide range of projects reveal that design and construction management fees generally represent less than 10 percent of total building costs. The remaining 90 percent is directly attributable to the hard, or direct, cost of construction.

Commodity pricing may be fine for assembly-line products but not for services that require human beings to exercise critical thinking. A/E/C management are not off-the-shelf products that can be packaged and sold like widgets. They are highly specialized, thought-intensive services that must be specially tailored to each construction project. The traditional sequential characteristics of design and construction projects involves architects and contractors at different phases of a project and with different responsibilities and contractual understandings; this often encouraged many owners to regard these services as mere commodities and to base their selections on low prices from a short list of firms that meet the minimum qualifications. Rarely did these owners realize the ramifications of forcing inadequate fees on design and construction professionals, who must limit their services and investment in a particular project in order to remain profitable and competitive. During the early stages of a project, including the selection of the professional team, clients should be encouraged to focus on value and not merely on price.

The new APD strategies that share risk and responsibility among architects, contractors, and often owners, are a collaborative force that combats this "low price" mentality. As a marketer, you must learn to educate the owner on the importance of a project team's ability to control overall project costs as well as their ability to provide quality work. The following are some points which a marketer should make potential clients aware:

- Successful cost control on an A/E/C project is the result of teamwork by all involved parties.

- If fees are higher but include services to better manage overall costs and quality, the owner may benefit by spending more in the initial stages of a project in order to reduce costs in the field construction stage.

- In A/E/C services, the issue of costs generally comes down to paying greater fees for greater talent and additional services. Selecting a firm (or team) that offers lower costs often means the client might be served by less capable professionals or by entry-level employees.

- The firm or companies selected should guarantee that no "bait and switch" of employees will occur after the contract award in order to meet commodity pricing of services.

- Most importantly, professional services should not be sold as a commodity. Clients will defer pricing issues only if they perceive that they will be getting better value from you than they would from your competitors.

Bonding Rather Than Selling

Private owners and major corporations have begun to align their facility objectives with their business objectives. Acquired real estate holdings either become profit centers in and of themselves or they manage their holdings at the lowest possible cost to prevent deterioration of corporate profitability.

The A/E/C industry must respond to these new realities, and implement the programs necessary to align the facility needs with clients' business objectives.

To do this, team members may be asked to participate financially in the future success of their client, deferring some of their initial fees and compensation for possible profit-sharing after the client becomes established. As more and more communities offer financing to lure businesses to their areas, A/E/C professionals are likely to be required to participate in these assurances to facilitate the sale of industrial revenue bonds.

Commitments for assistance start earlier and end later. Post-construction services are now common, particularly among manufacturing clients who demand that the entire building team participate in the turnover and start-up stage of their operations to ensure a smooth transition to the profit-making stage of all projects. Clearly, the trend in construction is leaning toward performance contracts rather than simply the completion of a building, to plans and specifications. APD strategies facilitate this development, in which successful marketers become partners, not just vendors.

Risk Transference

During the past decade, construction industry customers increased their use of risk transference to other parties, typically through legal advisement. Transferring risk was presumed to be an effective contractual means to reduce exposure to risk during a project's construction by assuring that an owner would not have to pay for risk allocation.

In reality, though, the opposite is true. Architects and contractors have transferred their assumption of risk to their subcontractors and consultants, and all parties may attempt to apply increased compensation costs to assume risk, thereby increasing overall project costs.

The risks associated with professional services should be retained by the organization being paid to complete these services. This is particularly true for all risks associated with construction designs. In the typical design-bid-build (DBB) contracting method, the owner is required to assume all risks associated with the preparation of the drawings and specifications, guaranteeing to the contractor that the design is free of errors and omissions (E&O). Recently, clients have realized that design risk should in fact be retained by the architectural and engineering firms that are being paid a fee for these professional services.

This situation has led to the substantial increase in APD projects, where the risk is shared by the members of the contracting team and not just individual A/E/C firms. In this way, clients are assured that all professional risks associated with the design are retained by the design and construction professional. As a marketer, you should be aware of how and when risk should be transferred, and should be sufficiently experienced in these issues to know when a potential client is requiring the team to assume too much risk to ensure a profitable project.

Staying the Course: Marketing Principles That Will Never Change

Although marketing has changed and will continue to change, some standard principles will never change, especially those relating to customer relationships. The technology that allows us to contact and communicate with a customer may have changed dramatically, but the manner in which customers should be treated will never change. You should become familiar with several enduring marketing techniques: (1) marketing versus sales; (2) perception is everything; (3) some customers are best ignored; (4) treat clients as friends; and (5) know your customer.

Marketing Versus Sales

Today's new realities demand that an architect or contractor not only maintain their standard operational departments but also maintain, at minimum, a sales or business development staff with the ability to perform marketing functions to increase the number of opportunities identified for sale closure. Moreover, the distinction between a "hard" technical staff and a "soft" marketing staff has broken down; today everyone in your firm has a responsibility to retain and generate business.

There is a difference between marketing and sales, despite the fact that many A/E/C companies manage them as one operation, usually within the business development department. Although the same employee can be responsible for both marketing and sales, management and business development staff should recognize the differences between the two functions. The best way to describe this intended difference is to use an analogy: If marketing is a war, sales are individual battles during that war.

Marketing is the plan of attack or the road map that succinctly develops the program that you as a marketer intend to follow during a certain period of time. Marketing embodies the process that develops the sales contacts that turn into contracts. Marketing is general; sales are specific. A marketing program includes planning to attract business opportunities in a new geographical area or specific type of work, and is structured to ultimately result in specific sales opportunities. Marketing programs include planning processes that position a company to be recognized as a solution for its targeted client's needs. Once identified as a possible solution, the firm's sales process starts to sell the company's services to this identified client.

In design services, marketing would begin with a strategic plan and a mission statement that structures a program to communicate to prospective clients. The process reverts to a specific sales opportunity when a contractor receives an inquiry from a potential client. For an engineer, architect, contractor, or any other person involved in providing professional services, establishing a direct-marketing mailing program or creating a company blog are key elements of the marketing process, whereas preparing a proposal for a client is the sales process. The contact with this client between the initial response and the request for proposal is likely to be a combination of marketing processes: providing a general qualifications package to supply further information, as well as a personal sales call to discuss the client's planned project. As there are many aspects of marketing, one can take this many steps further. Any contact with a client or potential client is a marketing task, even if it is the receptionist's handling of a telephone call or the accounting department's handling of an invoice.

The line between marketing and sales often becomes blurred, but there is nothing wrong with this because effective marketing programs should naturally evolve into sales calls. Everyone in business development should recognize that marketing and sales are ultimately both used to increase sales opportunities for the company. Unfortunately, many A/E/C firms have no marketing programs, relying instead on a sales effort that too often exists only as an estimating department.

Although it is not mandatory for a small architect or general contractor, for instance, to create a separate marketing and sales department, it should be understood that effective sales calls begin with a clearly defined marketing program that identifies appropriate customers for the company's long-term goals. It must also be understood that every person working for a firm should be considered a marketer.

Perception Is Everything

The way a person or company is perceived has always been a critical factor for successful marketing programs. In today's virtual environment, perception is even more important. In fact, it means everything.

The age of digitized communication and APD strategies has created the virtual firm, an organization that exists only to complete a certain task; this organization then dissolves and is recreated when another need arises. By establishing a website, a person can create a company (or team) through posted documentation but have no actual employees or experience. This kind of company will hire temporary workers only when an order is received from a client. Otherwise, the company does not physically exist, even though potential clients of this virtual company perceive it as an actual operating entity.

Perceptions can be based on fact or fiction, and individuals can perceive another person or company any way they please. Perceptions, once formed, are very difficult to change, regardless of whether they are right or wrong. For example, a person might make a first visit to a department store, be treated unkindly, and conclude that this entire department store chain is poorly managed based upon this one encounter. It is very unlikely that this perception will ever be changed. That same person might then express this view to others who have not visited the store, and influence their attitude toward the store before they have even had an opportunity to form their individual opinions. It is a recognized fact that although a satisfied customer might not generate more business, a dissatisfied customer can cause a serious loss in revenue simply because people are more likely to communicate their disappointment than their approval. You have heard the statement that a dissatisfied customer will tell ten people, who will tell ten people, who will tell ten people. Run the risk of having poor service and before you know it, your reputation as a company to be avoided will have traveled far and wide.

As a marketer, you establish the proper perception of your company by using the numerous means of communications available today. For perceptions to be positive and projects to be considered successful on completion, the architect, designer, or contractor must recognize that marketing is a continuing process that cannot be ignored. Communication with clients through established contact with the marketer, and additional visits when deemed necessary, are critical in creating a positive perception in the marketplace.

Some Customers Are Best Ignored

In every business, there are customers whose patronage a company is better off doing without. Every marketer should be able to recognize when it is appropriate to discontinue marketing to a specific client and abandon attempts to finalize a sale.

Too often, a sale is completed even though the marketing or sales representative recognizes that this client will probably not benefit the company and should not be solicited for contracting opportunities. Be wary of clients who: (1) emphasize price only; (2) fail to recognize the value of services provided; (3) have a history of litigation or create a hostile work environment; or (4) have insufficient financial resources.

Clients who emphasize price only will never become repeat clients because every project they contract for is selected on the basis of low bid and low price. A marketer should never waste company resources and funds to market to a client who is interested only in price and not quality.

Clients can certainly use low-bid contracting effectively to pre-qualify A/E/C companies, but those industry clients who are interested only in "getting something for nothing" are best left to competitors. Marketers should recognize that potential clients who are preoccupied with price issues never produce profitable long-term business relationships. These clients fail to recognize the value of services provided and treat professional services as a commodity. Be wary of the client who is unaware of the value of professional services.

The clients we speak of are also likely to create a hostile work environment. They not only minimize the importance of the project and the skill it takes to create it, but also take for granted the value of the human beings who are responsible for designing, building, administering, and completing the project. So poor is their regard for the people involved, they think nothing of changing the scope of the project at various stages of completion. Thus, change requests instituted by the client become extensive and unprofitable bargaining sessions.

It should be mandatory for every marketer to investigate and confirm the ability of a client to supply the necessary financial resources to complete the project successfully. Spending company time and resources to market to a client who has limited financial resources and is incapable of bringing a planned project to completion, only results in wasted time and effort for the marketer. As early as possible, the marketer should determine the client's financial commitments to the project. It is not unreasonable to inquire into the financial support for the planned project before investing estimating time, pre-construction services, and other support requested by the client. Marketers should be prepared to decide if the company they represent has the capacity and experience to satisfactorily complete work for the client and to finance it during an extended process.

All too often, marketers do not think of qualifying the potential customer, which is an important requirement. Any marketer or salesperson is, of course, intensely focused on "making the sale." However, it is dangerous to be so hungry for the sale that one overlooks the possibility of a sale "going sour." It is important that a firm's representatives recognize and distinguish a good opportunity from a negative situation. The negative impact from just one financially bad project can negate the success of several good projects. The margins in A/E/C projects are too small to take unnecessary risks, and expert marketers must be just as capable of rejecting risky opportunities as they are of closing good sales.

Treat Clients as Friends

Always remember that people buy from friends or people they know and trust. Competition is not based only on technical skills, price, and experience levels. Very often, a sale is made because of past friendship. Friendship counts—in fact, it wires the job!

You must recognize that marketing begins well before a project is planned or announced to the public. Clients are more likely to deal with architects or contractors with whom they have forged a relationship based on previous knowledge of their needs and with whom they have previously worked. Marketers who create a good working relationship with the client will certainly be awarded the majority of that client's work, even in situations in which multiple proposals must be solicited in order to satisfy corporate regulations.

Successful marketing is not just about submitting the best proposal; the best marketers recognize that many projects are sold long before the proposals are submitted. Use strategic planning to identify potential clients, and then build a friendly relationship with those clients to earn their trust. Doing this before you submit proposals is the key to successful marketing relationships.

If you want to establish a relationship based on trust and friendship, you should abide by five very specific rules:

1. *Never forget a customer or let a customer forget you.* Marketing is based on consistently renewing existing relationships and on forging new ones. Through the process of personal contact, mailings, calls, and digital marketing, a marketer must remind customers about the A/E/C professional's ability to help them achieve their goals. Marketers should never give the impression that they have abandoned the client once the contract has been signed; a good marketer will keep in constant contact with every existing client throughout the entire project process.

2. *Take care of your clients and they will take care of you.* When clients believe they are being treated fairly and professionally, they are likely to return that treatment to the practitioner. Remember these adages: What goes around comes around. Don't burn your bridges.

    A bad relationship can hurt you forever. Suddenly, in a new project, you encounter an old client with whom you have parted on a sour note. The old disappointment will rankle for a very long time, and you should expect that he might make a negative remark to someone standing nearby. Most clients belong to industry associations in which information is exchanged. No marketer wants a past client to repeatedly spread negative valuations to potential future clients, either when they are networking with their peers or when they have been contacted as a reference for qualification and technical submittals. Make amends with potentially dissatisfied clients, no matter what you have to do.

3. *Existing clients are the best source of new business.* A satisfied client should be used as a reliable source for new business leads. Clients are certainly aware of their competitors and what is happening in their industry, and this information can help you learn which companies might be planning new projects, expansions, or renovations, sometimes long before they are publicly announced.

    In addition, clients can also provide contacts within other industries through friendships and business associations. A referral or personal introduction can immediately open doors and form stronger relationships that might not otherwise occur.

At the very least, a satisfied client can be used as a reference for other potential clients. Never forget the opportunities that existing customers can provide beyond work with their own organizations. To be effective, you should use these relationships strategically to create other relationships and generate more business, as well as to focus on helping as many people in your own network as you can. This is called networking, and it has been the lifeblood of business and relationships from the beginning of time.

4. *Never forget the word "thanks."* Too often, marketers, in their zealousness to close a sale and move on to the next potential lead, forget to thank a client for awarding the project to their firm. Never forget to express the company's appreciation for a contract. Make sure the client recognizes that you will be available throughout the project's progress and continue to follow up with the client to ensure that they are satisfied with the services provided.

   Everyone respects and appreciates working with people who are sincere about expressing gratitude for the opportunity provided. Even if a practitioner isn't successful in obtaining a particular contract, sending a letter thanking the client for the opportunity will be greatly appreciated, and that client will certainly remember your courtesy when it's time for the next project. Never leave the client with the impression that the contractor did not appreciate the invitation to compete for their business. In today's world, this courteous gesture is seldom practiced by most professionals, or by most people in general; if you do this, it will ensure that you will stand out from the crowd.

   Sincere appreciation is likely to result in future opportunities and will go a long way to establish you in the mind of a prospective client as a friend or partner. Take this one step further, if you want to boost your career to the very highest level. When you see an article or notice in a newspaper or other periodical that will affect this client (or any other with whom you do business), clip it, put it into an envelope (or attach it in an email), and send it to him with a handwritten note. "I thought this might be of interest to you." Watch your reputation as a professional and valued friend zoom!

5. *Reciprocate whenever possible.* Everyone is in business to make a profit. Marketers must recognize that their clients are also required to sell work to stay in business. Marketers, whenever possible, should pass on appropriate leads or business opportunities to their clients. Nothing can cement a relationship better than providing a business opportunity for a client or anyone else you know in business. Sharing information makes you just as important to the other person as she is to you. No one will continue to share leads and information with people who do not reciprocate. Passing on information when appropriate is an important part of marketing or any business relationship. It permits the establishment of a network group that is crucial to the success of any marketing program.

These simple marketing practices can create a solid foundation for success for any marketer. The philosophy behind these principles is that to succeed, you must remember those who are responsible for your success. While you are the driving force in your own life, without the acceptance of your clients, you go nowhere in this market, or for that matter, in any work environment.

Know Your Customer

Just as important as establishing effective relationships with customers by getting to know them on an individual basis is gaining knowledge of their business and future goals. Helping a client become successful is the ultimate goal of any marketing program and in turn helps marketers achieve their own companies' goals.

Only by spending the time and effort to learn a client's goals and requirements can you provide the assistance that may result in long-term relationships. Meeting with a prospect only to boast of your firm's capabilities is useless. She can easily learn what your capabilities are. The question in her mind is can you solve her problems? Can you find solutions to a dilemma? Can you achieve what she has in mind? Can you envision the goal she sees? You must emphasize the value of the services your company can provide rather than emphasizing price issues.

Offering to become involved early in the planning stages of a project and providing input that increases the value of the completed project and the client's profitability is more valuable today than being the lowest bidder. Going a step further and offering suggestions to maximize a client's investment in physical building requirements can be the determining factor that will set your company apart from any of your competitors.

The most successful A/E/C service marketers set themselves apart by first learning everything they possibly can about the client's business, goals, and planning process; and then applying this knowledge to help the client make the right decisions for his project requirements. (How you learn about a client and his needs is a critical challenge and is discussed more explicitly in Chapter 4.) Once a potential client recognizes that you can provide assistance based on a thorough knowledge of not just A/E/C services but of his specific industry as well, that client will likely respond by inviting you and other representatives of your company to join the planning process and, eventually the implementation of the project.

With this technique, you succeed in moving the discussion away from commodity pricing issues and toward recognition of professional services. Construction firms can use this knowledge of the client's business and issues to sell pre-construction services to provide a competitive advantage for the construction phase. But if you really want to succeed with a prospective client, you need to do more than understand his or her needs. A good marketer demonstrates empathy with the client's challenges. Some industry experts even argue that this ability to emphasize with the client, what they term your emotional intelligence (EI), is more powerful than traditional notions of intelligence (IQ).

Knowledge of the client is also critical for responding to a client's technical proposal requests. Rarely do clients give you sufficient information in proposal requests for you to recognize what is actually expected in their proposal. Generally, the Request for Proposal (RFP) is terse, with dry, technical language. It is simply a blueprint in words of what is essential to the project. If you go by the details of the RFP and reply in kind (which is what you must do), what you will end up with is a proposal that will be a duplicate of everyone else's proposal – directed specifically to the details of the RFP and not recognizing what may be behind the RFP. If you are able to immerse yourself in each of the businesses of your prospective clients, you will be infinitely more effective in understanding their true needs than marketers who merely pass information along about their companies' capabilities.

This client-based knowledge is one reason why many larger A/E/C organizations separate their marketing programs by client industry type, and arrange to have their marketers specialize in a certain type of industry. This allows them to become more effective, both for the client and for the practitioner. For example, an architecture or construction firm might have some marketers targeting health care organizations, some targeting manufacturing corporations, and still others specializing in commercial development. Specialization permits marketers to concentrate on one particular type of industry, enabling them to learn not only customer needs but general industry needs as well. This specialization enables marketers to become considerably more effective in helping their clients become successful, and ultimately the practitioner shares in this success. If you become an expert in a particular field, everyone in this field will call upon you.

Although the way A/E/C firms operate may have evolved somewhat, one thing never changes: the way a client should be treated. This basic principle must be incorporated into every marketing plan or initiative.

Are These Immutable Marketing Principles Nothing More than Common Sense?

You may think that this discussion seems oddly familiar, that these marketing axioms are not much more than good behavior, the lessons your parents taught you and that were imparted so humorously in Robert Fulghum's *All I Really Need to Know I Learned in Kindergarten* (Ballantine Books, 2004). Just remember, the design and construction industry is built on relationships. Your word and your reputation are paramount. You can sabotage yourself with bad behavior far more quickly than you can repair broken trust. But while these basic marketing principles are necessary to do your job effectively, they are not sufficient by themselves. You must also understand the powerful new paradigms of the virtual project and alternative project delivery, which will be explored in-depth in our next two chapters. ∎

Things to Think About

- Will my firm's marketing strategies recognize the implications of the virtual project?

- How can my firm best take advantage of different collaborative opportunities?

- Is my firm succumbing to commoditization pressures?

- How can my firm improve its customer relationships?

CHAPTER TWO

The Virtual Project

Things You Will Learn From This Chapter

- How the dynamics of the A/E/C industry will impact how you promote and secure new business for your firm.

- How clients' expectations for A/E/C firms are changing.

- How rapid technological advances are creating opportunities for differentiation between A/E/C firms that can utilize new technologies properly and those that can't.

A/E/C MARKETERS SHOULD THOROUGHLY FAMILIARIZE themselves with how the business of architecture, engineering, construction, and related services is changing. These issues must then be incorporated into marketing programs to assure clients that the designer or contractor is capable of meeting the challenges of today's business environment.

Thanks to the influx of international resources and competition, the design and building industry is no longer a local or regional business. Technological advances in the design and building industry have flourished in recent years, and the use of digital resources is becoming a necessity. As project teams demand greater communication both in the office and in the field, the need for up-to-the-minute project updates calls for technology that supports all facets of a project's life cycle. New software, advanced communications, and virtual collaboration are all driving firms to venture beyond their current niches in order to remain competitive.

The combined impact of these three rapidly developing trends—design and construction technology, globalization, and electronic communications—has transformed the A/E/C industry from a relatively slow and linear paper-based process to a massively parallel series of instantaneous digital transactions, free of traditional constraints on place and time. The pace of this change will continue to increase for the foreseeable future, so it is vitally important that you understand how it affects your firm's capabilities, your competitors' positioning, and your clients' expectations.

How This Came To Be

In the years following World War II, the A/E/C industry prospered by serving the dynamic growth of developed economies around the world. But the industry remained, at its core, a fabric of relatively small businesses working locally or regionally that relied on traditional processes and means of communication. In those days, mail and hand delivery were the only ways to exchange documents; and a telephone, typewriter, and sometimes a blueprint machine were the only technologies needed to support a perfectly respectable and successful company.

As the economy began to shift from its roots in agriculture and manufacturing to an increasingly urban, office-based work force, innovations were being developed to support an expanding group of customers that directly impacted A/E/C firms, which prompted the dramatic evolution of technologies and delivery systems we are experiencing today. A timeline of key milestones, and their transformative influence on A/E/C includes:

- *Photocopier:* In 1959, Xerox™ Corporation introduced the photocopier, eclipsing carbon paper and making fast, multiple copies of small format documents an expected deliverable on projects.

- *Fax Machine:* In 1964, Xerox™ patented a way to use telephone lines to send a facsimile of a document (i.e. a "fax"). This technology mash-up between phone and copier compressed the days required by the postal service to deliver a document into seconds, immediately changing expectations for multi-party information exchange of "8 1 /2 x11" documents and making the fax machine a must-have technology. Large format drawings, however, still needed to be hand-delivered or mailed.

- *Overnight Delivery:* In 1971, a business school project based on the fundamental premise that time is more important than money led to the launch of Federal Express, further undermining the former dominance of the postal service and raising the bar on expectations for fast A/E/C document exchange in any size or format. From that point on, clients expected that any document, sample, or part from anywhere in the world would be available in less than 24 hours.

- *Design and Construction Software:* Throughout the 1980s, mass adoption of the personal computer for business spawned the development of a vast array of software programs to automate design and construction processes. This enabled more work to be done in less time and changed clients' expectations regarding multiple iterations, ever-faster turnaround cycles, and higher quality graphic presentation materials.

- *Printing/Plotting:* Increasingly affordable printers and plotters that quickly generate high-quality color renditions of the outputs from new software programs further enhanced the speed and efficiency of document-based processes. This also established an expectation that color deliverables in any size can be easily available on short notice.

- *Disk/CD/DVD:* Storing and exchanging the amounts of electronic information being produced on projects among A/E/C team members began with floppy disks and slowly transitioned to more robust CD/DVDs, although both formats still required physical transfer between parties.

By the mid-1990s, 50 years after the end of World War II, all of these innovations had become standard tools in A/E/C firms, establishing a baseline for clients' expectation for speed, accuracy, and quality of deliverables. But as important and transformative as these incremental advances were, the most critical turning point took place in 1995 when what had begun decades before as a restricted network of supercomputers called ARPANET was officially decommissioned, and what we now know as the Internet, was opened for commercial traffic. Since then, the explosive growth of email, instant messaging, Voice over Internet Protocol (VoIP) calls, two-way interactive video calls, file transfer (FTP) websites, and information available on the World Wide Web has exponentially accelerated the pace of technology-driven change taking place in the A/E/C industry. Add to that the sweeping global expansion of wireless technologies in the 21st century, and capabilities that were unimaginable even 20 years ago, an "always on" connectivity is now an expectation for everyone in the industry around the world. Your firm is part of this fast-changing transformation affecting all of the A/E/C community. You can differentiate yourself from competitors by taking effective advantage of emerging technologies and processes, and the business opportunities they present.

Building Information Modeling (BIM)

Although A/E/C technology steadily advanced throughout the 20th and into the 21st centuries, the industry is still primarily revolved around drawings (plans, elevations, sections, details) that were two-dimensional (2D) abstractions of the proposed design, supplemented by text in the drawings (notes, dimensions, schedules, etc.), and in separate documents (specs). Woven in among the developments in design software since the 1980s, however, was an interest in expressing design in three-dimensions (3D), in a way designers imagined it in their minds, and integrating the graphical and non-graphical information more seamlessly. What you now know as Building Information Modeling (BIM) grew out of that initiative.

At first, simple 3D visualizations were created by software that interpreted geometrical and dimensional information from 2D plans. Over time, though, sophisticated A/E/C software developers began taking advantage of advances in design and production technology from manufacturing industries, where intelligent digital objects of parts and components containing both geometric information and performance, and material data are combined to virtually "build" a highly realistic visualization in order to fully refine its design prior to physical production. This digital model also directly controls factory production equipment to ensure repeatable, reliable accuracy and consistency.

BIM first gained traction in Europe during the late 1980s, and then in the US and Canada in the early 2000s. It is now one of the fastest growing technology trends in the A/E/C industry. Research by McGraw Hill Construction shows that in 2007, only 27 percent of A/E/C companies in North America were working on projects on which BIM was being used by at least one of member of the project team. Five years later, that number jumped to 71 percent. As technology adoption advances, so does the percentage of each company's projects involving BIM. McGraw-Hill forecasts that by the end of 2014, 40 percent of the A/E/C industry in North America will be involved with BIM on over half of their projects, with less than 20 percent having no BIM involvement at all.

Using BIM software on a project is not mandatory. You can also use virtual coordination (a.k.a. "clash detection"), which leverages models created by multiple other companies, or have other parties create models of your work that end up benefiting you and the project. Once BIM is introduced on a project, however, almost everyone involved engages in some meaningful way with the digital version of the design or the models developed by builders, fabricators, and installers to guide their processes.

The Virtual Project

Key among the trends that have emerged from the growth of BIM is the concept of the virtual project. Because BIM uses digital data from intelligent objects instead of unintelligent lines, arcs, and text, almost every aspect of a complex design and the building process can be modeled, analyzed, iterated, simulated, evaluated, and optimized on computers before a single purchase order is issued or a shovelful of earth is turned on the site. This "digital double" of the physical project has quickly proven to be invaluable, and is becoming a standard element of the A/E/C process. Additionally, owners are increasingly demanding as-built models after construction for ongoing facilities management and operations; a demand that provides new design, construction, and service opportunities for your firm. *(See Example 1)*

Example 1: *ASU Morph with iPad.*

Impact on A/E/C Services

Real-time, up-to-the-second information is available at a person's fingertips around-the-clock. Constant communication creates a business environment that never sleeps, and a competitive environment that requires firms to innovate and collaborate to create the best possible product.

The A/E/C industry is rapidly increasing its use of technology in the office, on the construction site, and is designed into projects. Smart buildings incorporate building automation systems to react to changes in weather, foot traffic, lighting needs, maintenance issues, and an abundance of other variables that require facility maintenance. These automated systems are interwoven into a building's infrastructure, which is tied back to the preplanning, design, and construction phase of a project. Automated systems can also be monitored on mobile devices, thereby allowing remote facility maintenance. For example, a building in California can have its air conditioning turned on by an individual in New York who is monitoring the building's HVAC system.

Video conferencing and webcasting have broken down barriers that engages collaboration across geographic boundaries. A firm's offices and partners can meet on the spur of a moment even if they are located thousands of miles away from each other. Live design charrettes are able to take place without each team member physically being in one location, and those charrettes can incorporate new design technology to showcase what-if scenarios, as well as capture planning information at the same time.

Virtual construction structures a corporation with complete electronic connectivity for each individual construction project; it involves partnering with individual organizations required to complete a particular project. Virtual construction capability is centered on the client rather than being based upon the usual hierarchical organizational chart, allowing the client to interact with the entire team directly and instantly. Virtual corporations (meaning the teams selected for a particular project) exist only as long as necessary to complete a particular task. Upon completion of the task, the virtual corporation ceases to exist until another task is required and another team is assembled to complete it. The entire far-flung group of team members may be supervised by a single individual in a single cubicle with a single computer or by a small group of people linked by computers.

Technology Advancements

As we discussed at the beginning of this chapter, there have been a number of key technological advances that have accelerated the pace of change, and creating new ways to deliver projects and serve clients. Your firm needs to be aware of how these advances will impact your business.

BIM's Effect on the Industry

BIM is the single most transformative influence currently impacting the A/E/C industry. Once a project is modeled (meaning once it has been developed in a BIM program rather than a CAD program), its physical and functional characteristics are documented in a digital form rather than a purely graphical one, as happens with CAD. This means that various team members can access whichever specific parts of the overall database they need to perform the task is at hand.

Major ways in which BIM is changing the design and construction process and affecting clients' expectations include:

- *Analysis and Simulation:* Designers and builders now have access to software that will quickly and efficiently run analysis and simulations on modeled projects and allow different scenarios to be compared for faster and better decision-making. This can include:

    - Analyzing energy performance based on factors such as different site orientations or the amount and type of glass in the building envelope.

    - Simulating human interaction with the completed environment, for example, to test emergency exits or to make sure a facilities engineer can actually perform the maintenance that will be required on building equipment.

    - Simulating various construction sequencing scenarios to determine in advance which one will be most efficient, and then using BIM's visualization capabilities to communicate the appropriate sequence to the clients and individuals who will be doing the work.

❑ Evaluating constructability of proposed design solutions in advance of implementation to make critical adjustments and prevent delays or expensive changes necessitated in the field.

These types of analysis and simulation generate better and more reliable solutions, providing enormous value to clients. As such, they have become standard operating procedure for modern A/E/C companies, and are one of the top reasons why your firm needs to be fluent in BIM.

- *Integration with Schedule (4D) and Cost:* Since a model is composed of intelligent objects, information relating to the schedule for on-site arrival and installation of a component, as well as that component's cost, can be linked to the object. Integrating the schedule with the model is known as 4D. With these digital connections in place, the project team can understand the full scope of the project in 3D, as well as its detailed plan for execution and its cost at a granular level. Changes can be managed more efficiently and the budget and schedule can be managed with more reliability and certainty. This is a great benefit to clients, and they are likely to expect that your company will be able to provide this level of service.

- *Spatial Coordination and Model-Driven Prefabrication:* One of the most popular and valuable uses for models is the virtual identification of any geometric conflicts between the various building systems (the primary ones being architecture, structure, mechanical, electrical, plumbing, and fire/life safety). This process, referred to as coordination, was traditionally done using transparencies of 2D drawings physically laid on top of each other on a light table, and was painstakingly reviewed by experienced staff. Now if these systems have been modeled, software programs can automatically find any conflicts. This virtual process has come to be known as "clash detection" and is probably the most commonly conducted BIM process when multiple systems have been modeled. *(See Example 2, p. 33)*

Because trade contractors trust the coordinated model, they are now willing to prefabricate parts of the project that were formerly done piecemeal, thereby greatly accelerating the project completion process. Much of this work is now being done off-site, with large assemblies being sent to the site and installed, rather than built at the site from raw materials. Under this system, shop labor typically makes up about half the cost of field labor, working conditions are safer and more pleasant, there is far less material waste, and final quality is generally better and more reliable. This important shift toward model-driven prefabrication is enabled by the spatial coordination made possible by BIM, and the resulting impact on quality and project duration is changing clients' expectations about project delivery.

- *Visualization:* Because all the physical information about a project is held in the BIM software as data, any view you can imagine can be rendered on demand, and animations or sequences can be captured as videos. Models can also be integrated in other programs, such as Google Earth, to place a project in its actual context. This powerful visualization

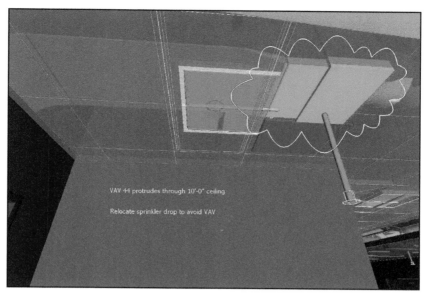

VAV 44 protrudes through 10'-0" ceiling

Relocate sprinkler drop to avoid VAV

Example 2: *Spatial Coordination and Model-Driven Prefabrication.*

capability has had a profound impact on the process of communicating anything and everything about a project, from site massing alternatives to high-resolution renderings for client presentations to animations of multiple construction sequences to very close examination of specific details for construction. Clients now expect visualizations that rival those they have come to expect from movies and TV.

RFID, GPS, Lasers, and Augmented Reality

In addition to the specific advances in design and construction technology, many other industries are driving technological development and growth that impact our industry as well.

- *Radio Frequency Identification (RFID):* Small chips attached to objects emit tiny radio signals so that their location and information can be detected by hand-held devices. Name badges, toll tags, and merchandise all include RFID tags. The cost of these devices have come down to the point that construction projects now routinely use RFID to manage material deliveries and on-site materials and to update installation progress in real time. For example, Skanska used RFID tags in their supply-chain process to track pre-cast pieces on the MetLife Stadium project. RFID also allows facilities management to quickly locate and access information about components or equipment, although battery life in the chips currently limits that use over time.

- *Global Positioning System (GPS):* Beginning in the 1970s, the use of satellites to improve navigation was becoming standard. Using this new system, any point on the surface of the earth or in the air above it can be assigned X,Y,Z coordinates that will locate that point three-dimensionally within a 1/16 of an inch. Models can contain GPS coordinates for any component to be installed and new tools can identify that precise location in the field at any height off the ground, greatly expediting construction processes and increasing accuracy.

Example 3: *First Baptist Church Dallas Sanctuary Points and Model.*

- *Laser Technology:* Initially envisioned by Albert Einstein in 1917, lasers have become commonplace throughout the developed world. In A/E/C, they have two main applications:

  - *Laser Scanning:* Massive numbers of laser beams (called "point clouds") can be emitted from a stationary device; when they are reflected back, the device can calculate the exact distance to every surface that was struck by each beam. In this way, an image of an existing space or structure can be calculated with extremely precise geometric accuracy. *(See Example 3)* These laser scans can be uploaded into BIM software to quickly generate a model of any existing condition at a level of detail that was impossible to achieve through manual surveying and measuring. Not only is laser scanning the most effective way to do "reality capture" of existing facilities, it is also frequently used during construction to capture as-built progress and compare it digitally to the intended design. This on-the-fly validation prevents costly rework and brings unprecedented certainty to project execution. Laser scanning is also a valuable tool during design and preconstruction as it offers data that may not have been historically captured in an existing project.

  - *Guidance:* In the field, GPS-enabled hardware devices can access coordinates from a model and emit a laser beam to identify a precise spot for builders – for example, on a slab where a penetration needs to be cut or on a partition where a component should be installed. This precision guidance gives a distinct competitive edge to companies that have learned to deploy it effectively.

- *Augmented Reality:* The entertainment industry has driven a number of advancements in visualization of virtual spaces for applications like gaming and theme park attractions, as well as movies that seamlessly blend live action with computer imagery. This digitally generated "augmented reality," in combination with modeled data and GPS coordinates, provides a powerful toolset for design and construction.

Designers can seamlessly simulate proposed design solutions that are integrated perfectly into video footage of actual environments, or a contractor can use a tablet to view actual partially completed construction through its camera function and visually access any aspect of the final design called up from the model to combine future state with present state in a single view. This is useful because it validates that all systems are properly installed in a wall cavity before applying sheetrock by viewing the final placement of the equipment, which will be serviced by those systems from the model, in a partially completed space.

Each of these technological innovations from other industries has raised the bar for speed, accuracy, and quality, and as such, they are fast becoming must-have elements in every A/E/C firm's portfolio of tools and capabilities.

Tablets, Wireless and Mobile

As computers become smaller, more powerful, and more mobile, the A/E/C industry is responding with new and modified approaches to connect with and work on these devices. Every company is wrestling with how to take advantage of these changes in the most economical way. Some major general contractors provide hundreds of tablets to their field staff to ensure that models and project management data are accessible on-site, while companies are taking more of a wait-and-see attitude.

It is clear that the use of computers of various kinds has many benefits. McGraw-Hill Construction's research on *Information Mobility in the Construction Industry,* published in October 2013, shows that the majority of the contractors surveyed report strong improvements in collaboration and productivity and that there is a growing trend toward less reliance on paper-based plans and specifications. Median schedules and cost reductions were reported in the nine percent range, although these benefits were enjoyed by a higher percentage of large firms and the required investment was cited as an obstacle for smaller companies.

What Technology Advancements Mean to Your Company

The continuing integration of design and construction disciplines, and the inevitable shift away from paper to digital information-based processes makes using these emerging technologies is not a matter of "if," but of "when." Your firm not only needs to have a technology strategy addressing which systems make the most sense for your business, but you also need to convey to your client how these technological advances serve as a competitive edge. *(See Example 4, p.36)*

Internal Improvements

Although much of these technological influences have been external, many other advances in construction products and services have come from within the industry. A/E/C companies are focusing more on innovation in design, software, and processes. For example, with the advancement of lighter steel, structural engineering firms are able to design award-winning buildings like HL23 in New York City. Prefabricated shear wall panels saved the project time since the majority of the work was done offsite and the wall panels could be spliced in the field.

Example 4: *Sample of visualization from digital model of complex tunnel.*
(Source: Parsons Brinkerhoff)

Several companies have created their own proprietary software for use in the office as well as in the field. Civil engineering firms created GPS tracking systems to locate site landmarks like utility lines, and property management companies have developed 3D modeling systems utilizing laser scanning images that can locate piping behind closed-in walls and pinpoint maintenance issues. Other companies have created in-house software development departments in order to create and innovate as quickly as the A/E/C industry evolves.

Better processes are also being derived from innovation. Lean design and construction stems from the automotive manufacturing industry, and adapts design processes to reduce waste (including materials, time and effort) in order to create the best possible outcome. Project teams utilize lean design and construction best practices in order to communicate expectations, lead times, knowledge, challenges and successes through regular meetings and interactive charts. These processes help build trust among team members, and give everyone common goals for the project.

Subcontractors' Roles

Operating in the virtual world precludes an organization from operating in a vacuum isolated from suppliers and customers. To meet clients' demands for virtual scheduling and instant gratification, designers and contractors must be connected with all team members and, in particular, with subcontractors and trade contractors.

Few contractors today are true general contractors, performing all the work on a project themselves; rather, they act as construction managers and subcontract the majority of the work on a project. Subcontractors have become the niche experts within the industry, providing the technological knowledge for a specific building trade. This knowledge must be incorporated into the early phases of project planning and design to meet clients' demands for faster and better delivery of the construction project. As technical experts in their specific niche markets, subcontractors can directly assist design firms in selecting products and components that enhance the overall design. By making pertinent suggestions about what can be done to reduce construction schedules and costs, this process can help improve the overall quality of the finished product. The participation of subcontractors in early planning is even more critical for design-build contracting, an alternative project delivery strategy that we will address in the next chapter.

Cloud Computing/Real Time Data/Advanced Communication

Documentation in the A/E/C industry has always involved huge amounts of paperwork: site plans, architectural drawings, as-builts, contracts, receipts, accounts payable, etc. Firms still keep some hard copies of these documents, but most now utilize electronic storage filing. Cloud computing allows firms to store these documents on remote servers, yet still allow access to the files over the Internet.

BIM files can be very large and can consume a firm's internal computer server space, thus slowing down the network and hindering the proficiency of the project team. In addition, large files are hard to share between companies. Cloud computing allows multiple parties to access large files so that any member of the team can manipulate the design, add notes and comments, and update the file without draining the firm's internal computer server. This type of file sharing and storage allows for real-time data transfers, which happen throughout the life cycle of a project's design and construction. New technology can model buildings, associate material costs, and assign scheduling within a few seconds so that all project stakeholders know what the construction costs are projected to be moving forward. It also allows those stakeholders to modify different project variables (design, material costs, cut and fill adjustments, etc.) to get the best possible project outcome.

Email is second nature to nearly everyone in the A/E/C industry. Project sites use email for communication, and many are also starting to use mobile communication pods that include web casting, remote server access, and field offices. Video imaging allows remote team members to view the project site and to assist with real-time solutions. Server access and cloud computing portals allow project managers to quickly validate project specifics by pulling up BIM files.

Time Compression

Today, everything moves faster. Clients are under pressure to finish projects in ever-shorter timeframes, which trickles down to all members of the project team. The traditional design-bid-build (DBB) process is under extreme compression, with fast-track quickly becoming the norm, and there is less room than ever for errors because errors cost both time and money.

Any technology you can adopt to reduce the incidence of errors by increasing certainty and to shorten project duration by improving efficiency, will be a competitive advantage for your company.

Getting to "Yes" Faster

Traditionally, design firms allocate a specific portion of their fee to the design process. This process is not over until the client approves the design for documentation, which can take much longer than originally anticipated. A delay of this kind can place a firm in a negative financial position that is difficult to recover from. Powerful visualization tools that quickly and effectively convey design solutions, paired with analytical and simulation tools that put more "science" behind design recommendations, can speed the whole approval process. *(See Example 5)* It can also create better alignment between clients' expectations, and the reality of the completed project. When clients are able to clearly visualize almost any aspect of a proposed design in high definition, not only are they more confident in their approvals, they also are more invested in the final outcome, becoming real members of the design team.

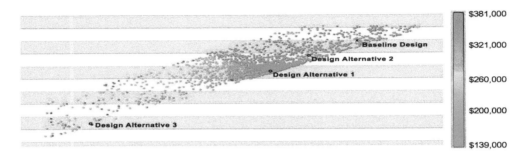

Example 5: *Optimization results from scatter plot.*

What Time Compression Means to Your Company

The pressure from clients to achieve more in less time is never going to abate. Rather than avoid this reality and seek to transfer the risk, it is better to acknowledge it and apply your company's resources to learning how to manage it. Clients are looking for innovative ways to compress project delivery schedules while maintaining control of cost and quality. Your firm has the opportunity to implement a number of technologies that give you unique capabilities to address this challenge.

Tomorrow's A/E/C Industry

Technology will be an increasingly important element in the A/E/C industry as it continues to evolve toward an integrated delivery process. The inevitable industrialization of construction will rely heavily on the speed, accuracy, and computational power of digital tools and processes. The following is a brief description of three key trends that will shape this industrialized A/E/C future.

Simulation and Analysis

While models are already providing these types of services, we are barely scratching the surface of the possibilities for simulation and analysis. These services will present a great opportunity for your firm to really differentiate itself as a team of great analytical thinkers as well as excellent designers or builders.

Immersive Visualization

Clients love to see proposed design solutions, and contractors need to see what they are supposed to build. Continuing advances in display technology, driven largely by the entertainment industry, will enable both clients and contractors to fully immerse themselves in a model or model-based simulation. *(See Example 6, p. 39)* It is important to be at the forefront of this trend because once your competitors provide this service to clients; it will set a new level of expectation and rapidly become mandatory for everyone.

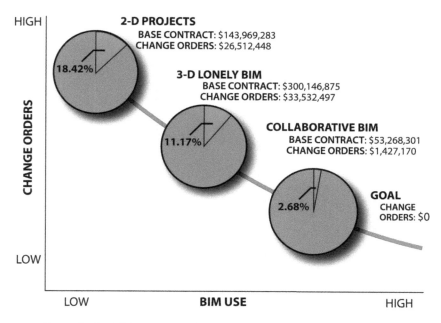

HIGH

2-D PROJECTS
BASE CONTRACT: $143,969,283
CHANGE ORDERS: $26,512,448

18.42%

3-D LONELY BIM
BASE CONTRACT: $300,146,875
CHANGE ORDERS: $33,532,497

CHANGE ORDERS

11.17%

COLLABORATIVE BIM
BASE CONTRACT: $53,268,301
CHANGE ORDERS: $1,427,170

GOAL
CHANGE
ORDERS: $0

2.68%

LOW

LOW   BIM USE   HIGH

Example 6: *Collaborative BIM—Change Orders Chart. (Source: J.C. Cannistraro, LLC)*

Productization and Modularization

Despite what A/E/C firms may want to think, clients are not looking to buy a bundle of services from a group of different companies, many who never worked together before, and all of whom are more interested in their own well-being than in the final product. What the client wants is a building, or a bridge, or a power plant. If it were possible, most clients would prefer to snap their fingers and have the asset quickly appear, ready to use and with a comprehensive owner's manual, like purchasing a car. Instead, they have to endure the prolonged and risky process of having their product custom-built.

This will change, as surely as it did with other major industries in which mass customization now dominates the design and delivery cycle. In the future, the A/E/C industry will rely on:

- *Productization*: For example, mechanical contractors who are repeatedly prefabricating multi-system assemblies like above-ceiling corridor racks for hospitals will take the next step and offer a catalog of predesigned racks based on their experience with hundreds of hospital projects. They will be able to easily make these on demand at a reasonable cost. Since the designs are based on solid experience, architects and engineers will be willing to specify them and design around them, as they already do with many building products.

- *Modularization:* Some companies, such as Casaflex in Mexico City, already have state-of-the-art factories that produce ever-larger components and assemblies. These companies can configure a complex project virtually from a pre-engineered kit-of-parts and assemble it quickly and safely on-site. Firms like Aditazz in California are addressing the same concept for specific verticals, in their case, health care.

Companies that you likely never heard of, or that may not even exist yet, will come to play a major role in this modular approach to project design and delivery.

What this vision of the future means for your firm depends on your willingness to innovate and embrace the business opportunities that these advancing design and production technologies provide. The change is unstoppable—some companies will suffer and some companies will thrive. The question for your firm is both simple and profound: Will you be among the survivors? ■

Things to Think About

- How can my firm respond to the continuing pace of technological change and turn it into a competitive advantage?

- How can my firm deliver our services in a more integrated process with other companies to more effectively meet our clients' needs?

- What kind of implementation process does my company have to get up-to-speed on new technology?

- How will design and construction technology affect the way I do marketing and business development?

- How will technology help better communicate our project goals to stakeholders?

CHAPTER THREE

Alternative Project Delivery:
Meeting the Owner's Project Demands

Things You Will Learn From This Chapter

- Why project owners are demanding alternative approaches to project delivery, including a perspective on the project owner's universal project expectations.

- A historical perspective on the classic master builder, and the evolution toward specialization of the designer and builder roles beginning in the 19th century until today.

- A comparison of the three most common forms of alternative project delivery and how they contrast to traditional design-bid-build.

- How and why alternative project delivery has grown in demand by owners and in practice by designers and builders.

- Details and formats of the fundamental types of alternative project delivery that dominate the marketplace.

- Which alternative project delivery models work well based on the owner's preferences and policies relative to project design and construction.

AS A PROFESSIONAL DESIGN AND CONSTRUCTION SERVICES marketer and business developer, you must adapt to and master key changes happening in our industry or eventually become irrelevant to your clients. You have the ability to go beyond the typical design and construction services and assist your clients with an array of other integrated services: risk management, sustainability, life-cycle cost control, and financial options, among others. Delivering your services in a way that addresses these more complex owner demands will not only give you an opportunity to do more business with your current clients; it will also allow you to out-distance your competition and generate new business opportunities.

Alternative project delivery (APD) lets you to respond to expanded owner demands. Over the last few years, APD options have become less "alternative" and more mainstream in their application. Today, about half of all commercial construction uses *Market Share by Project Delivery Method, Figure 3:1 (p. 46)* as an alternative to the traditional design-bid-build (DBB) project delivery system that has dominated the industry since the Industrial Revolution. You need to understand what is driving this change and how today's service providers can better position their staff and resources to meet this changing demand.

APD is really a generic term referring to project delivery models such as construction management (CM), integrated project delivery (IPD), and design-build (DB). While there are many alternative delivery models (in name and structure) to the traditional design-bid-build, they all have one overriding objective: They seek to better integrate the decision-making responsibilities of the project owner, designers, and builders at every level of activity and throughout the project's life cycle.

Why should we integrate? Owners are interested in pursuing alternative approaches to project delivery in order to better achieve the fundamental project expectations. They are transitioning from design-bid-build to APD because alternative delivery strategies are completing projects more quickly, more cheaply, and more safely. Price adherence, scope satisfaction, and a dependable schedule are chief among owners' top priorities. You assuredly have heard the questions, "What's it cost, what's it look like, and when do I get it?" Owners demand these answers not on a whim, but as a result of increasing demands placed on them by their leadership, constituents, and shareholders.

This chapter will discuss and examine a variety of APD's characteristics and issues, illuminate their underlying strategies, and address why the APD approach has gained increasingly broad acceptance by owners throughout our industry.

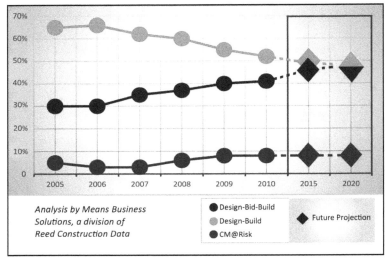

Figure 3.1 *Market Share by Project Delivery Method (Non-Residential)*

How We Got Here: A Brief History of Design and Construction

Our brief review of the design and construction industry's history begins in 1772 BCE when the Code of Hammurabi was set in stone tablets as the law of ancient Mesopotamia. One of the Code's laws mandated that the architect was responsible and liable for both design and construction decisions. Note that "architect" is translated from Latin as "master builder," one who guides design and construction. What this means is that full integration for design and construction, within one accountable and responsible entity, is actually the classic form of project delivery, preceding the traditional design-bid-build model by some 3,000 years.

By the mid-1800s, the notion of the master builder was lost due to specialization, a hallmark of the Industrial Revolution. Reflecting the growing division of practice between design and construction, the American Institute of Architecture was formed in 1857. AIA brought the art of design into focus not only as an activity but also as a product. As designers became separate from more tangible construction activities, design products shifted more to drawings and renderings. Over time, formal architectural education became focused on developing and documenting abstracted design ideas created in studios rather than constructed results at a jobsite. This is not to say that architects and engineers became completely isolated from the construction of their designs, but it is telling to that even today, several states do not require the designer-of-record to be involved in a project's construction.

The creation of the first trade unions during the same time period furthered trade specialization. The specialization of designers and builders, combined with advancements in manufacturing, transportation, and materials technology, pushed construction productivity to new heights. For example, Carnegie's production of steel allowed for long-span bridges and the first skyscrapers to be built. For the A/E/C industry, the 19th and early 20th centuries were a time of greatly expanding productivity that continued until the mid-1960s, after which time the industry has been characterized by significant ebbs and flows.

From Segregated to Integrated: The Spectrum of Accountability

To understand alternative project delivery, we must first understand the default project delivery method: design-bid-build (DBB). The principal characteristic of DBB is its sequential and linear approach to design and construction activities. It begins when the owner selects the design team (architect, engineer, specialty designers, etc.). This team, working closely with the owner, then creates and fully documents the project design using drawings and specifications, otherwise known as contract documents.

Following full documentation, the owner advertises the contract documents for the solicitation of bids (bid prices from the marketplace of builders). The owner then confirms the validity of the bids and awards the construction contract to the lowest responsible bidder.

Evaluation and selection of design professionals usually involves a measure of experience, knowledge, past performance, and references. Low price is commonly not a criteria for selecting architects and engineers, as required by the Brooks Act for federal contracting. Since architects and engineers are licensed professionals whose license is regulated for the purpose of protecting the life and safety of the public, price or fee cannot be the dominant criterion for their selection. A selection based on lowest price may erode the life and safety principle laid out in the Brooks Act.

As indicated by the Federal Register: "On October 27, 1972, the Brooks Architect-Engineers Act (92) (40 U.S.C. 541 *et seq*., re-codified now at 40 U.S.C. 1101 *et seq*.) required that all requirements for Architect-Engineers (A-E) services be publicly announced, and be negotiated on the basis of demonstrated competence and qualifications for the type of professional services required, at fair and reasonable prices. The Act established a specific qualification based procurement process to be used in procurements for architect-engineer services, which the Act defined as 'those professional services of an architectural or engineering nature as well as incidental services that members of these professions and those in their employ may logically or justifiably perform.'"

While the required professional services vary from owner to owner, generally those services include scope definition, bidding administration, and contract administration. Scope definition usually includes project programming (defining the owner's project needs) and design/documentation (documenting a solution/design within detailed drawings and technical specifications). Bidding for construction services involve publishing the drawings/specifications and collecting bid responses from the marketplace for consideration by the owner. Contract administration services affirm contract compliance (ensuring that the resulting construction is in accordance with the drawings/specifications), addressing builder's questions or Requests for Information (RFIs), and processing other administrative matters such as payment applications.

DBB is fundamentally a segregated, linear process. First the project owner selects the designer or design team and then the designer, working under contract with the owner, establishes the project program (the *problem* to be *solved* through design) and subsequently provides a documented solution (drawings and specifications). The solution is "put out to bid," and then those bids are tabulated, with the lowest responsible bidder being awarded the construction contract. As construction takes place, the design team, in service to the owner, measures compliance with the contract documents (drawings and specifications).

It is important to note that the designed solution (drawings and specifications) must be 100 percent complete because any missing, incomplete, or undocumented portions of the solution will not be included in the bid or the subsequent contract between the owner and builder. This is what gives DBB its character and name: design then bid then build. It is also why change orders are inevitable in DBB, as perfect drawings and specifications are as likely as flawless construction results—both activities are subject to human error.

In contrast, and as demanded by project owners' expectations (see *Figure 3.2, p. 49*), alternatives to DBB are growing in popularity because of their ability to integrate the entire design and construction decision-making process. Although it is an established tradition that is well understood by everyone in our industry, DBB tends to extend schedules and diminish communication by segregating the professionals (designers versus builders) involved in the decision-making process. Since the builder's adherence to the bid price is solely dependent on the clarity and completeness of the designer's drawings and specifications, and since the success of the designer's solution (encoded in the drawings and specifications) is ultimately dependent on the construction results, flawless communication is paramount to the owner's success. The simplest and most obvious way to strengthen communication between the designer and builder is to put them on the same team.

The Three Primary APD Models: It's All in the Contract

While there are some subtle variations among different APD approaches, they are all primarily subsets of three predominant models: construction management at risk (CMAR), design-build (DB), and AIA's integrated project delivery (IPD).

In the CMAR delivery model, the owner establishes two contracts: one between the owner and designer and another between the owner and builder. In this respect, CMAR emulates DBB: a dual-contract operation with which most owners are familiar and comfortable. However, CMAR differs from DBB in that the owner establishes these two contracts at about the same time, thereby allowing the builder to provide input during the design process. With CMAR, the owner's selection process is typically qualifications-based (as is the case with DBB), measuring the designer's and builder's experience, past performance, capacity, and skills.

CMAR allows the designer and builder to collaborate with the owner from the project's beginning. The owner, designer, and builder can jointly evolve the solution, balancing the impacts of scope, cost, and schedule. This joint evolution lays the foundation for a spirit of partnership, shared responsibility, and tighter coordination of a project's details.

DB goes one step further in the integration of project team members by joining the designer and builder in a single contract with the owner. The collaborative advantages created in CMAR are reinforced in DB by the use of this single contract. Since the designer and builder are contractually

Project Owners' Seven Fundamental Expectations

Upon hiring the project team (the owner's designer and builder), owners have expectations for performance. Often these expectations are not written down, but they most assuredly exist.

These expectations are in large part the reason that many project owners are searching for alternatives to the traditional project delivery model: design-bid-build (DBB).

As a result, any project delivery model must structure itself to respond to and meet these seven fundamental expectations:

1. *Be On Budget:* On budget means no surprises and no change-orders. With integrated project delivery and design-build, the contractor (service provider) is given design and construction leadership; thus, there are no more excuses.

2. *Satisfy Scope:* Irrespective of what is detailed in the design and plans, the final outcome must support the project's mission. Being in scope means meeting all of the documented requirements of the RFP, not only designing and building the project but also managing and ensuring a successful out-come.

3. *Meet the Schedule:* For most owners, the occupancy date is the key milestone. Many parallel operations (that may not always be apparent to designers and builders), depend on this date being firm.

4. *Be Professional:* Professionals have an obligation to do only what their skill and training will allow. Therefore the owner's project is not an opportunity to discover the solution; it's not an experiment, it's a commitment. "We didn't know, realize, foresee, understand, etc.," are not acceptable explanations.

5. *Be Predictive:* Predictive means that the service provider can (with certainty) predict the results of their decisions. If someone is professional (doing what he KNOWS), then by default he should be able to predict the results of his own decisions. Owners depend on this ability.

6. *Be Accountable:* If the service provider does not meet her obligations under the contract, then she must be responsible for bringing her services and products back into performance with no cost to the owner.

7. *Meet the Market:* The owner expects to receive a fair market price – neither the cheapest price nor the most expensive. This expectation requires the owner to know (discover) what defines a fair market price. Likewise, the owner expects to receive a fair market service. This is the basis for professional "Standards of Care," and the owner deserves nothing less.

Explaining the connections between a project delivery model's strategy and these seven expectations is one key to successfully marketing alternative project delivery.

Figure 3.2 *Project Owners' Seven Fundamental Expectations.*

a single entity, the owner does not need to settle any disputes between the two. This single-point of accountability, responsibility, and administration is a significant selling point for owners.

As with CMAR, the owner can use non-price factors in the evaluation and selection of the design-builder, including experience, past performance, skills, capacity, management approach, and so on. These non-price factors can be combined with price factors such as total price, unit cost, time/materials, etc.

IPD maximizes the integration of the primary project players: the owner, designer, and builder. Collectively, these three players form the project entity and, for all intents and purposes, all three have an ownership position. Developed by the American Institute of Architects (AIA), IPD can be seen as the ultimate integrated alternative delivery model. Since the owner, designer, and builder are all members of a joint venture, their motivations are directed toward the project's outcome rather than their individual positions. With IPD in general, all three players are partnered in their success or failure. However, because of this joint ownership position, public entities (such as government owners) are barred from such joint venture models.

As your firm begins to provide integrated design and construction services (APD), you have the opportunity to address two of your clients' most urgent needs: adherence to budget and quality of results. APDs provide better adherence to budget and overall project quality because they can provide better communication throughout the project's entire design and construction life cycle. Builders provide feedback to designers in real-time, while the design decisions are being made and drawings and specifications are being resolved. Designers then provide feedback to builders in real-time, while construction activities are being planned and implemented.

As a result of this integration and enhanced communication, team members can mitigate many of the risks that drive up costs by establishing an intimate working relationship between the owner, designers, and builders. Each decision related to developing the design, coordinating the construction, and commissioning the results can be discussed in detail with all of the team members. Concerns related to function, operation, practicality, constructability, availability of material and resources, cost, and schedule can be raised by any team member throughout the project. At the same time, integration of understanding makes the project's goals clear to all team members, allowing the team to capture many opportunities, otherwise lost, that enhance project results.

Although not all APD models eliminate final price and quality variations, some alternative delivery models, by allocating roles, responsibilities, decision-making control, and risk, can contractually guarantee the project's final price and performance quality at contract award for the designer/builder team (as will be discussed below).

Industry Productivity and Risk: The Downside of Chasing the Upside

Research has presented a number of theories as to why our productivity as an industry is declining. Risk is one such issue that has been identified as a primary cause. Risk comes into play for everyone involved in the design and construction continuum: owners, designers, builders, suppliers, manufacturers, and so on. While there is no universally accepted definition of construction productivity, most agree that it is a function of the resources consumed (labor, material, etc.) versus unit output (square foot, cubic foot, or other program metric) over a given timeline. Our industry's collective challenge is how to increase productivity (maximize final project value) without increasing the risks associated with higher/better output.

This challenge is what is driving APD: owners demanding more, with less time and fewer resources at their disposal. Traditional approaches to project delivery are being scrutinized by those on the supply side in response to the changing needs of those on the demand side. It is important to note that APD is not an original product thought up by designers and builders, but rather a response to owners' demands for better project results. Owners' expectations are more frequently missed through the use of traditional DBB and are therefore driving the demand to lower project risk by reinventing the project delivery process.

The Intersection of Innovation and Accountability: Risk Is Inherent in Any Given System

For project owners, risk resides primarily in three fundamental questions: "What does it cost, what does it look like, and when do I get it?" Change-orders are a poison for any owner; all of their financial success is tied to their budget forecasts. Scope and schedule needs take a backseat to the importance of the budget. Owners can often work with a little upset to the scope of their project, and a smidgen of a schedule delay can be accepted, but blow the budget and it's game over.

Marketing APD services is commonly done by contrasting APD to the traditional DBB delivery method, and various APD methods are often defined by how they allocate risk. This is done by describing the risk (cost control, schedule control, quality control, etc.) and assigning that risk to one of the entities involved with the project. For example, being familiar with DBB, you understand that the cost of the project is established by the design (designers design to a budget that, beyond the project cost, includes the builder's profit and their fee) and that competing builders set the price of the project. How well the bid price aligns with the budget is only discovered on bid day when the envelopes are opened. Riskier yet (for the project owner at least) is that the final project price is subject to change due to change-orders, among other things.

To explain the impacts of this risk on a project's outcome, the *Risk Profile Matrix (Figure 3.3)* demonstrates key relationships. Across the top of the matrix are the primary participants in any construction project: the owner, designer, and builder. The vertical axis identifies responsibility, the principal attributes of risk, control mechanisms, and control tools. This matrix can help you to visualize a project's interconnected relationships and how various project delivery models will affect such relationship.

Figure 3.3 *Risk Profile Matrix. (Source: 3PQ Acquisition & Management Systems)*

For example, the owner (owner's representative) is responsible for mission satisfaction: the operational needs that the finished project is intended to fulfill. The owner's shareholders (in the case of private sector entities) or the taxpayer (in the case of public sector entities) hold the owner accountable for satisfying this mission. The owner's activities focus on mitigating any risk that threatens the mission.

To mitigate risk, the owner translates the mission into scope. By defining what the project must be, the owner further mitigates the risk that the mission will not be satisfied (at least in the traditional

DBB model). To better define scope, the owner traditionally depends on professional design services that provide project programming and contract documents (drawings and specifications). In the matrix, mission satisfaction is tied to scope definition, and the scope definition is in turn tied to the quality, capacity, knowledge, and experience of professional designers hired by the owner.

The Request for Qualifications/Proposals (RFQ/P) is the control tool employed almost universally by owners. Once the designer is on board, he works closely with the owner to ultimately create the contract documents, otherwise known as the drawings and technical specifications.

In the same fashion, the designers' and builders' risk, control, tool, and responsibility are easily understood. Designers are at risk for errors and omissions (E&O) within the instruments of service, while builders are at risk for schedule adherence and personnel safety related to their construction activities. Although there are many subsets of risk for designers and builders, errors and omissions management (for the designer) and schedule and safety management (for the builder) dominate their respective approach to overall project management and delivery of services.

Designers mitigate the risk of E&O through the thoughtful design processes. The craft of design is instituted in the traditions of mentorship and internship. Designers (both architects and engineers) have a pace, sequence, and methodology to the development, consideration, and decision-making that goes into thoughtful design. Documentation of the design can further mitigate the risk of E&O; many designers adhere to conventions for the form and organization of drawings and specifications. For example, the Construction Specification Institute (CSI) has established a convention for specification documents based on construction trades.

Builders mitigate risks related to scheduling and safety though the orderly process of building. Similar to design, construction has a pace, sequence, and methodology inherent in the process. By controlling the means and methods (M&M) related to construction activities, the builder could mitigate the risks associated with schedule adherence and human safety.

Finally, each entity has a responsibility to the other: designers set the direction via design, owners verify that direction via mission understanding, and builders follow the direction via construction activities.

Risk and APD: Pinpointing Risk within Systems

Following the various relationships identified by the risk matrix, we can understand how various project delivery models seek to mitigate risk and what each model depends on for its success. Remember, the only reason that owners embrace a new project delivery model is that it may better satisfy their seven fundamental project expectations *(Figure 3.4, p. 53)*.

Consider design-bid-build. *Figure 3.5 (p. 53)* shows a black line between the designer and the builder. This black line represents the contract interface. As the contract documents (drawings and specifications) derived from the designer define the owner's required contract scope, the owner and designer are seen as one, left of the line. To the right of the line (the second of a two-entity contract) is the builder.

Based on the traditional DBB contract interface, the owner guarantees to the builder that the contract drawings and specifications are complete and without error. This is codified as the Spearin Doctrine,

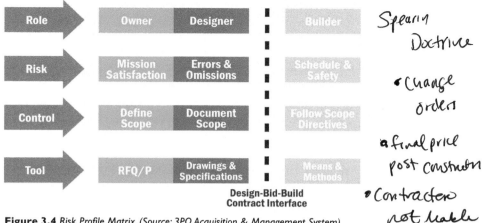

Spearin Doctrine

• Change orders

• final price post construction

• Contractor not liable

Figure 3.4 *Risk Profile Matrix. (Source: 3PQ Acquisition & Management System)*

which states that the contractor will not be liable to the owner for any loss or damage resulting solely from insufficiencies or defects in information, plans, and specifications. By contract, the builder follows the owner's drawings and specifications to the letter. Any error, omission, ambiguity, or other defect in the contract documents (drawings and specifications) that impacts the builder's schedule or cost constraints is resolved via a change-order for an adjustment to the contract. When using DBB, the owner generally must wait for the conclusion of all construction activities to know the final price.

The opposite extreme sets the contract interface to the left of the designer (*Figure 3.5*). This scenario establishes one contract between the owner and designer/builder (the designer and builder having their own contractual arrangement). In this relationship, the designer/builder or design-build contractor follows the owner's RFP Documents to create the solution, which is derived from the design and documented within drawings and specifications. The builder is not contractually obligated by the owner-furnished drawings and specifications; rather, the design-builder is contractually obligated by the owner-furnished RFP Documents.

One contractual agreement

RFP based

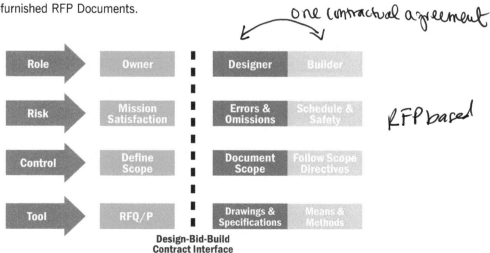

Figure 3.5 *Risk Profile Matrix. (Source: 3PQ Acquisition & Management System)*

What is unusual for our industry is the content of the owner's Request for Proposals (RFP) documents. Under this design-build approach, the RFP documents must detail and describe all the measurable criteria that the ultimate solution (both completed design and built construction) must satisfy. Since the design-builder controls the tools of design and construction unilaterally, he also controls the design and construction decision-making process. Combining this unilateral control (again, under the Spearin Doctrine) is why the design-builder is liable for all risks (design errors and omissions, as well as errors in construction means and methods) associated with satisfying the owner's RFP requirements.

Since they no longer control the project's outcome via drawings and specifications (this responsibility now residing with the design-builder), owners must add far more performance detail to their RFP documents, as they are the basis-of-scope and the contract documents that replace the traditional drawings and specifications. It is important to note that this change in how and by whom the design is controlled accounts for much of the angst and confusion surrounding design-build as an APD model; designers, builders, and owners have yet to settle on a standard RFP document convention.

CMAR

We will now look at the structure related to another popular APD: construction management at risk (CMAR), also known as construction manager/general contractor (CMGC). CMAR maintains the dual contract relationship of the owner with both the designer-of-record and the builder-of-record and creates a high level of coordination and collaboration between the designer, builder, and project owner. Similar to DBB, CMAR allows for direct control of design decisions by the owner, since she maintains a contract directly with the designer. CMAR also greatly enhances the builder's understanding of the required construction by including him directly in the design and design-review process. The builder's involvement and associated role at the design phase of the process provides a higher level of quality control, better understanding, and more accurate probable-cost information for the owner.

While design-build allows for setting a final price at contract award, the CMAR delivery model usually sets a guaranteed maximum price (GMP) for the project when the drawings and specifications are around 30-50 percent complete. CMAR establishes the GMP from consideration of the drawings and specifications (to date), along with stated conditions and limitations of understanding related to the GMP. Unlike DBB and DB, since the contract price is a GMP, the contract administration follows an open book approach for the accounting of project costs related to the final price; savings are commonly shared between the owner and CMAR contractor. By contrast, both DBB and DB are commonly contracted on a fixed-price basis.

There are many other contract possibilities that can be mapped on the risk matrix. Bridging-based design-build partially replaces the owner's RFP performance criteria with conceptual drawings and specifications. These conceptual (or bridge) designs are the basis of a contract in which the design-builder (different designer) completes the design and provides the construction services to completion. If bridging documents are contractually obligated, then the Spearin Doctrine can come into play and cloud the risks associated with design and construction. Many owners are attracted to this APD method because it maintains their direction of design while allocating some design responsibility to the design-builder. In practice, bridging-based design-build requires details within the contract that clearly allocate the risks associated with the owner-designer and the design-of-record.

The final APD model removes any contract interface from the matrix. The American Institute of Architects has created documentation for integrated project delivery, or IPD. In this case, integrated project delivery is not a conceptual process, but rather a unique contractual structure in which all members of the matrix (owner, designer, and builder) enter into a formal partnership with each having a vested interest in the project's successful completion. IPD seeks ultimate integration and collaboration by creating a single entity for the project, as if an owner were designing and building the project for himself.

IPD focuses on the single entity absorption of risk, in contrast to DB's focus on the dual entity allocation of risk. The obvious question is who (owner, designer, and builder) controls and shares what percentage of risk in the context to the partnership; the AIA provides literature with recommendations for how to address this question (for more information, see Additional Resources).

One Potato, Two Potato, Three Potato, Four: Choosing the Right APD

As a marketing and business development professional, you have a myriad of owners' perceptions and misconceptions to navigate when promoting APD. Likewise, you have a myriad of internal personalities to unify when pursuing APD projects. Perception is often reality, so changing (or enhancing) your firm's or client's perception of roles, responsibilities, and decision-making control can be the major roadblock to successful APD adoption.

Many owners will be interested in APD if they can understand the direct links between their fundamental project expectations and the attributes of various APD models. Much of the research and empirical and anecdotal evidence compares and contrasts APD to the traditional DBB delivery model; see *Figure 3.6* for a visual comparison. DBB attributes are shown in gray and represent a baseline for comparison. The figure's black cells represent improvements how the indicated attribute can be reliably achieved. Finally, white cells represent a diminished opportunity to reliably achieve the attribute. Using this matrix, you can determine which APD aligns with your owner's expectations, comfort level, internal resources, and so on. Designers and builders can also use this matrix drive a conversation about which APD skillsets align with their own mission and business model.

APD requires a different way of thinking and responding to project delivery. As the risk matrix discussed previously indicates, APDs result in significant shifts in how various responsibilities, tools, and liabilities are structured. Understanding and navigating these shifts is critical to delivering the improvements suggested by the matrix in *Figure 3.6 (p. 56)*. For example, let's suppose that due to funding commitments, an owner is interested in knowing the final price for their project as early in the acquisition process as possible. Based on this single attribute, we note that DB provides the best opportunity to provide this final price commitment early in the project acquisition process.

Since you are marketing APD, the use of tools such as the delivery model comparison matrix will allow you to discuss your firm's APD services in the context to your owner's project delivery needs.

Natural Extensions to APD: Advanced Integration

Because of APD's collaborative and integrated service approach, turnkey alternatives create an almost endless array of the services you can provide. As a marketing professional, you now have

Owner risk as comparison to D-B-B (Traditional) Method of Project Delivery	Design-Bid-Build (DBB)	Construction Management at Risk (CM-R)	Multiple Prime Contractors (MP)	CM Agent using Multiple Prime Contractors (CM-A)	Integrated Project Delivery (IPD)	Design-Build (DB)
Owner Considerations						
Adversity to change order	0					
Owners ability to make timely key decisions	0					
Ability to reduce gaps between services	0					
Simplify call backs and warranty issues	0					
Owner Schedule						
Timing to establish definitive project scope	0					
Timing to establish definitive construction cost	0					
Ability to fast-track the project	0					
Total project duration	0					
Owner Control						
Owners desire to control design details	0					
Owners desire to control project outcome	0					
Desire to have control of all prime contractors	0					
Increase in project transparency	0					
Increased ability for high performing projects (LEED, etc.)	0					
Project Budget						
Adversity to Change Orders	0					
Need to establish budget at earliest possibility	0					
Reduce the duplication of services	0					
Least cost for value received	0					
Owner Relationships						
Direct relationship with designer	0					
Select entire team not just designer	0					
Ability to establish a more professional relations with contractor	0					
Desire to avoid adversarial relationships	0					
Ability to increase project coordination	0					
Ability to reduce project claims	0					
Owner Communication						
Single point of contact	0					
Importance of having construction input during design	0					
Ability to negotiate cost and scope	0					
Ease in reaching an equitable contract	0					

Figure 3.6 *Owner Risk Comparisons to D-B-B.*

the impetus to explore the needs of your clients more deeply and the strategies and collaborative capability to address those needs.

Your client's sustainable and green building initiatives are a natural fit for APD. APD models strengthen integration by bringing together people and resources that go far beyond simply a designer and builder. This collaboration can easily address issues that may not have previously been considered basic goals of the design and construction process. The team approach, central to APD models, allows for collaboration with specialists to solve your client's need for energy and water efficiency, environmental stewardship, LEED certification, operational efficacy, or any other subordinate outcomes sought by clients.

Extensions of DB include design-build-operate (DBO) and design-build-operate-maintain (DBOM). Thus, owners can have their mission needs satisfied for any and all phases of a project's service life. Not only can the owner have the project designed and constructed for a set price (design-build), they can have their mission needs met on an ongoing price-for-service basis. DBOM can establish a monthly or annual price for service, akin to a lease. For example, some municipalities can pay an annual price for the treatment of water or wastewater. The agreement establishes the quantity and quality performance metrics of the facility, usually with a service life buyout date on which the ownership reverts to the municipality.

Public-Private Partnerships: Alternatives to Include Financing

Financing can likewise be an additional service that fits naturally with APD. Many public projects in need of project financing options to get off the ground are being delivered using APD models. Again, APD's natural collaboration allows for the easy integration of finance partners into the delivery team.

Public-private partnerships, or PPPs, are an effective strategy behind large public projects such as bridges, major highways, water and wastewater projects, and other public interest development projects. These partnerships bring together a public owner and a private designer and builder, along with a mix of public and private financing conduits that fund the project. As risk allocation is a fundamental component for this type of team structure, APD provides natural collaborative framework.

The National Council for Public Private Partnerships (NCPPP) has this to say about public-private partnerships and project delivery: "A Public-Private Partnership (PPP) is a contractual arrangement between a public agency (federal, state or local) and a private sector entity. Through this agreement, the skills and assets of each sector (public and private) are shared in delivering a service or facility for the use of the general public. In addition to the sharing of resources, each party shares in the risks and rewards potential in the delivery of the service and/or facility."

The NCPPP has developed several best practices for PPPs, recognizing that the methodology for the implementation of PPPs can vary depending on the nature of a given project and local concerns. Key elements of these best practices include the following.

1. *Public Sector Champion:* Recognized public figures should serve as the spokespersons and advocates for the project and the use of a PPP. Well-informed champions can play a critical role in minimizing public misconceptions about the value of an effectively developed PPP.

2. *Statutory environment:* There should be a statutory foundation for the implementation of each partnership. Transparency and a competitive proposal process should be delineated in this statute. However, unsolicited proposals can be a positive catalyst for initiating creative, innovative approaches to addressing specific public sector needs.

3. *Public sector's organized structure:* The public sector should have a dedicated team for PPP projects or programs. This unit should be involved from conceptualization and negotiation through final monitoring of the execution of the partnership. This unit should develop Requests For Proposals (RFPs) that include performance goals,

not design specifications. Consideration of proposals should be based on best value, not lowest prices. Thorough, inclusive Value for Money (VfM) calculations provide a powerful tool for evaluating overall economic value.

4. *Detailed contract (business plan):* A PPP is a contractual relationship between the public and private sectors for the execution of a project or service. This contract should include a detailed description of the responsibilities, risks, and benefits of both the public and the private partners. Such an agreement will increase the probability of the partnership's success. Realizing that all contingencies cannot be foreseen, a good contract will include a clearly defined method of dispute resolution.

5. *Clearly defined revenue stream:* While the private partner may provide a portion or all of the funding for capital improvements, there must be an identifiable revenue stream sufficient to retire this investment and provide an acceptable rate of return over the term of the partnership. The income stream can be generated by a variety and combination of sources (fees, tolls, availability payments, shadow tolls, tax increment financing, commercial use of underutilized assets or a wide range of additional options) but must be reasonably assured for the length of the partnership's investment period.

6. *Stakeholder support:* More people will be affected by a partnership than just the public officials and the private sector partner. Affected employees, the population receiving the service, the press, appropriate labor unions, and relevant interest groups will all have opinions and may have misconceptions about a partnership and its value. It is important to communicate openly and candidly with all stakeholders to minimize potential resistance to establishing a partnership.

7. *Pick your partner carefully:* The best value (not always lowest price) in a partnership is critical in maintaining the long-term relationship that is central to a successful partnership. A candidate's experience in the specific area being considered is an important factor in identifying the right partner. Equally, the financial capacity of the private partner should be considered in the final selection process.

If Nothing Else, APD Enhances Your Business Approach: Alternative Low-Bid

After understanding the advantages of APD, you might be wondering what is to become of the traditional DBB process. It's not likely to go away for some time because many public and private sector clients still accept it. The strategy of pursuing the lowest price, even at the risk of sacrificing some measure of value, still appeals to many owners, although that number is decreasing.

If your firm still implements a considerable amount of DBB services for valuable clients, selecting pieces of the APD strategy can improve your relationships and give you a competitive advantage. For example, encourage your owners to accept pre-qualification statements as part of an overall strategy to increase project value. Often pre-qualification is supported by the public (the critical constituent in public projects) as it safeguards their tax dollars; it also allows you to demonstrate an integrated and collaborative approach to construction, working with the design-of-record, and satisfying the owner's overall project goals.

The poet Maya Angelou noted that, "We all do what we know, and when we know better we do better. But we always do what we know". In the end, as a marketing and business development professional, you are the front door to your firm. The client largely understands your firm's story as presented by you and as interpreted by their own experience. Advancing your firm's APD portfolio begins by telling a story you both know. ∎

Things to Think About

- Why has APD grown in demand and acceptance?

- Is the designer or builder a better leader of APD?

- What draws the individual owner to APD?

- Other than traditional knowledge of design and construction, what are the required skills of an effective APD service provider?

- Why would an owner, designer, and builder have different perspectives on a particular APD model approach?

- How is APD different, or the same, as the services you currently provide your marketplace?

CHAPTER FOUR

Market Research: Know Yourself, Your Client, Your Competitors

Things You Will Learn From This Chapter

- Why market research is critical to your firm's success.

- The three-legged stool for marketing your firm.

- The basics of a SWOT analysis.

- The basics of competitive intelligence gathering.

- How to use the web for market research.

THE PREMISE OF THIS CHAPTER IS SIMPLE: For you to succeed as an A/E/C marketer, you must be able to differentiate your firm's capabilities from those of your competitors. You must have a solid understanding of the needs and challenges of your current and prospective clients, and you must recognize the strengths and weaknesses of your competitors. The good news is that in our digitized universe, you can often find all the information you need. There is no longer any excuse for you to pursue a client with their unspoken objective not showing up in the request for proposal (RFP). Similarly, you will have no one to blame but yourself if you underestimate the strengths of a competitor's strategy for a client's project that you really want.

In other words, market research is key to your success. As Sally Handley, president of a New Jersey-based marketing consulting, training, and staffing firm, has observed, the goal of market research is "to smooth out the peaks and valleys of both marketing and operations." Used carefully, this research will prepare you to market aggressively and successfully. You have a wealth of resources, easily used, to obtain the research data you need. But before discussing how best to use these resources, you must first develop an overall data collection strategy. What will you do with this information?

The Three-Legged Stool for Marketing Your Firm

Having the best product or the best service is no guarantee for success. As a marketer, you must analyze every opportunity on three distinct, but complementary, levels. First, you must be able to identify the unique services that your firm can offer. Second, you must truly understand the specific needs of your potential client. Third, you must recognize and then adjust your strategy in light of your competitor's strengths and weaknesses.

Know Yourself

How well do you know your own firm? A potential client typically is not interested in when your firm was founded, how many employees you hire, or the number of branch offices you have. These are all features of your company, but they have no direct relevance to the potential project you are trying to corral. The client wants to know what specific, concrete benefits they will get if your firm is hired.

Your ability to clearly describe your firm's benefits to the client is critical. Simply put, what will your firm bring to the project that no one else is able to offer? If you cannot articulate these benefits, you are tacitly admitting that your firm is not the best for the job. You might be among a number of qualified firms, but clearly you are not the most qualified!

To gain confidence in your skill in explaining your firm's benefits, practice your "elevator speech." Pretend you are in an elevator and you have 30 seconds to make your case to a potential client until the elevator stops at his floor (60 seconds if you are in a tall building). Practice until you can confidently describe your firm's benefits in 30 seconds. Actually, you should always have at least two elevator speeches prepared: one describing your firm in general terms and the other making the case for why your firm should be hired for a particular project. Working on your elevator speeches will force you to identify what really makes your firm different and how you can confidently and authoritatively articulate that to anyone.

You should also know how your firm is perceived. Conducting a perception survey is a powerful way to determine what people think about your firm and the value you bring to the marketplace. Based on the results, you might uncover strengths that you had not thought of before.

Know Your Client

Far too many proposals are lost because the bidder did not really understand the needs and challenges of the potential client. If the first time you think about a client and his project is when you read the RFP, RFQ, or other mass release, you will likely lose the project to a firm that did more advance research. Knowing your client's needs and unspoken objectives will not guarantee a win, but it is a necessary first step.

Networking is a strategy that you must enthusiastically embrace, and there are many types. As Ford Harding, author of *Rain Making: Attracting New Clients No Matter What Your Field* (Adams Business, 2008), and other key marketing texts explains, networking demands that you build and maintain a high level of trust with your prospective clients. There are numerous ways for you to understand their needs more fully and to develop a relationship of trust:

- *Nurture your current clients.* As you work on and complete a project, take time to speak with your clients and discover their major concerns. What do they like about your firm's service? What are they worried about? How can you make life easier for them? Remember, it is much easier to get repeat business with an existing, happy client than to secure a project with someone with whom you have never worked. You like familiarity, and your current client may like it as well.

- *Remain on close terms with former clients.* Even though a project may have ended two years ago, you should continue your relationship with former clients. They may not have any work for you at the present time, but if you continue to have a positive relationship, you will be able to learn about their future needs and challenges. Whether the discussion gets specific about a potential new project or just stays on the generic level of their projected needs, you will have captured intelligence that most of your competitors will not have.

- *Never eat alone.* Make it a practice to have lunch once or twice a month with someone whom you do not know and with whom you are not doing any business. At a minimum, you will expand your social/business circle and might learn about a new trend, product, or service. Perhaps your new luncheon acquaintance will become a friend; in the best of all worlds, this lunch-mate might become a future business partner or client.

- *Invite potential clients to your conferences, webinars, and other special events.* If someone in your firm is presenting a webinar on a topic that you think might interest a potential client, invite them to attend. The worse thing that can happen is they will decline, but you may still score some points for making the invitation. Perhaps you could co-author a paper on a topic of mutual interest with an individual whose firm you were targeting for future work. Consider reading an article on a new trend that you found interesting; take an extra few minutes to email the article to some of your contacts who might find it interesting as well.

- *Walk downtown.* Sometimes you may become aware of a project, or the need for a project, by stumbling across a vacant lot or a half-finished building. Make the effort to leave your office and observe what is going on in your neighborhood and community.

- *Go to city council meetings.* Many discussions regarding zoning, permits, easements, and a host of other issues are presented in public meetings. You may just become alerted to an issue that your firm is particularly well-positioned to solve.

- *Join relevant trade and professional associations.* This is probably the easiest way to expand your professional circle. It is also an opportunity to enhance both your reputation and the visibility of your firm.

- *Check out your clients' media presence.* You might start with their website, but look for content everywhere: LinkedIn, Facebook, company blog, Twitter, etc. This review should give you great insight into their most important concerns. On Twitter, for example, you could note not just the content of their most recent feeds, but what companies, agencies, or individuals they are following. If you read something that resonates with you, respond and interact with them.

Know Your Competitors

You cannot pursue projects in a vacuum. No matter how well you define your firm's benefits for a particular client and no matter how well you know and understand that prospective client, you will rarely get a client without any competition. If you have convinced the client to offer you a sole-source, uncontested project, congratulations! Your networking paid off. But in the vast majority of cases, you will have competition.

Although in some instances a competitor will come out of nowhere, in most cases, you should have a good idea of which firms are pursuing the same projects as you. Most of the time, these competitors will be qualified to complete the work. Your task, then, is to demonstrate to the client that choosing your firm is the only possible option.

You can only do this if you have a realistic understanding of both the strengths and the weaknesses of your competitor. How do they compare to your firm in terms of specific experience on comparable projects? Have they worked previously with the prospective client? How does their staffing compare to your firm? If you are able to answers these questions, you will then know how to develop strategies to pursue the project. Your entire approach, from your initial capture strategy to the specific written proposal and finalist interview, will then take both strengths and weaknesses into account. Without mentioning your competitors by name, your strategy will be improved, because you will know where their soft spots are and how you can address them.

Planning a Research Program

Now that you have developed a framework and strategy to better know your firm, your potential client (or more broadly, potential market), and your competitors, how do you develop an effective research program? Whatever your strategic plan, there are many excellent research methods available to you. Staff development, competitor research, market expansion, personnel background checks, monitoring market shares, keeping up with the latest trends and developments within your segment of the building industry—all of this and more can be organized by your firm. However, before you go surfing and following random leads, save yourself some time and create a work outline.

Identify the specific information for which you are looking. Are you thinking of moving into a new market sector? Will you consider delving into a different geographic area? Brainstorm with fellow staff, existing clients, prospective clients, and local trade associations. Prepare a list of potential sources from which to obtain the statistics and data you need. Gather the information and organize it by topic and subtopic. After you have gathered a significant amount of information, meet with your office staff again, review the information you have found, try to identify the areas that need additional support, and see if there are new areas to cover. Continue the search process to fill in the blanks. Meet again with your company team to assimilate the information, summarize it, and determine whether a conclusion can be drawn. Recognize that the information you have assembled will resonate differently with each individual in the group; each may offer a different and valuable interpretation and may offer you information on where you can find additional important details. Use this checklist:

1. Identify information.

2. Brainstorm with staff and others.

3. Prepare a list of resources.

4. Gather and sort the information.

5. Meet with staff again. Determine what's missing.

6. Continue the search.

7. Meet with the staff again, review information, and get input.

Start developing your strategic plan based on the research you have gathered and the input of your colleagues. Research takes time and labor, but the results will be focused and based on fact, not just your intuition. These results can provide the direction needed to make the serious decisions necessary for creating a strategic plan with the real potential to improve your bottom line. Such a plan will provide an organized road map for you to use to collect and analyze information, as well as timetables to follow to achieve the end product. Ultimately, your plan will help you make better marketing decisions.

The driving goal of all research is to help your company increase its revenue. A company that is about to undertake a marketing research project of any size is well advised to consider, during the initial planning sessions, its strengths, weaknesses, opportunities, and direct market threats, otherwise known as a SWOT analysis. Such an analysis provides a method for the team to systematically review the internal and external elements that have a direct influence on a company's success. *Figure 4.1* provides a sample SWOT analysis.

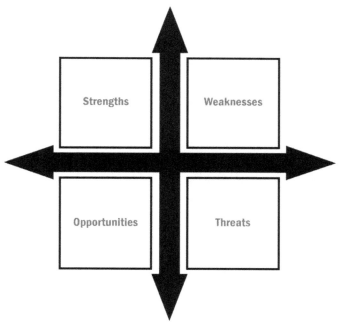

Figure 4.1 *SWOT Analysis.*

Strengths

- ■ Average experience of individuals in the firm is eight years.

- ■ Expertise in stadium structures.

- ■ Repeat business with 75 percent of client base.

- ■ Able to adjust to changing market conditions.

Weaknesses

- No marketing plan has been developed.

- Limited experience in a new major market segment.

- Large number of new employees with no experience.

- Low repeat business ratio.

Opportunities

- No direct competitor in institutional market segment.

- Successful completion of current work in a new market area.

- Strong networking ability within regional associations.

Threats

- Three new firms moving into the area with specific market experience

- Low unemployment rate

- New procurement methods to which the company has limited exposure

Once a SWOT analysis has been accomplished, the process will become simpler. However, as research takes inordinate amounts of time, do not start in the middle of your busy season. Plan ahead and begin the process when you have the time to devote your full attention to this important task.

Set priorities and proceed systematically. Try not to take on too much at once. Assign portions to your staff and support personnel, and establish your priorities. As you go about your regular daily assignments, meetings, preparation of estimates and proposals, and general problem-solving, you may encounter pieces of the research puzzle to be added.

Research Options: Primary and Secondary Research

Primary research is when you acquire data first-hand, rather than being gathered from published sources. Some of the methods a researcher uses to acquire data include in-person interviews, focus groups, telephone surveys, or self-administered mail surveys. Primary research is particularly useful for gleaning attitude and opinion data. For example, you may conduct a perception survey to understand what clients and prospects think of your firm, or you could develop an internal perception survey to gauge staff attitudes about your firm and its future growth strategies.

This approach may yield some very specific data, but can be relatively expensive to complete. If you have not performed primary research before, you may need to hire a consultant. Survey wording and ordering must be consistent and unambiguous; a poorly defined problem or an inadequate sequence of steps to uncover the information will not bring the right answers.

There is no "best" survey method. Each survey type has its strengths and weaknesses in terms of cost, response rate, ease of administration, and other variables. *Figure 4.2* compares some of these survey methodologies.

Survey Type	Response Rate	Cost	Advantages	Disadvantages
Mail-In	Low	Moderate	• Few Advantages when compared to other survey types • E-mail increases effectiveness	• Return rate ≤15% • May increase data entry • Focused on quantitative info
On-line	Moderate	Low-moderate	• Easy to administer • Easy data analysis • Can reach many people easily • Potential high ROI	• More focused on quantitative information • Some on-line programs are costly unless used often
Telephone	Moderate-high	Moderate-high	• Can incorporate quantitative & qualitative info • Allows for follow-up questions	• Time-consuming to administer • Can be costly depending on who administers
In-person	High	High	• High yield of qualitative information • Can strengthen relationships	• Time-consuming to administer • Can be costly • Challenging to schedule
Focus Group	Low	Moderate-high	• High yield of qualitative information • Allows for follow-up questions	• Time-consuming to administer • Can be costly • Challenging to schedule

¹ **Responsive rates: Low = ≤ 25%; Moderate = 25-50%; Moderate-High = 50-75%; High= ≥ 75%**

Figure 4.2 Survey Methodologies from *Marketing Handbook for the Design & Construction Professional, p. 35*

Secondary research uses material that has already been collected by another party, whether by government agencies, foundations, private firms, industry journals, trade magazines, or list brokers. This option is generally less expensive than primary research, but you have less control of the data since someone else conducted the data collection.

Competitive Intelligence Gathering

Effective marketing requires intelligence gathering and research. All firms have some form of marketing information database system in place that connects the external environment with the company executives, but it is even more important to provide this link at all levels of the organization. Research must have input from everyone and must be shared by everyone to be truly effective. Leave anyone out of the information loop, and you have rendered that person ineffectual. Full participation is key to success.

A good marketing information system should be divided into four parts:

1. An internal reports system provides current data on accounts receivable and payable, sales, costs, executions, margins, and cash flow.

2. A research-gathering marketing intelligence system is one that supplies executives with everyday information about what is going on in the external marketing environment. This can range from reading the newspaper to accessing a website for a projection of current projects, with a breakdown on what they are, who owns them, who is building them, and where they are located. A well-trained marketing and

sales team can obtain data from an online resource, hire a marketing consultant, or utilize its staff for special intelligence gathering activities. This can greatly improve the information that company executives receive.

3. A marketing research system involves collecting information that has been targeted for research because of a perceived threat to or opportunity within the company. This process takes five steps: (1) defining the problem and thoroughly narrowing the research objectives; (2) developing a marketing research plan; (3) gathering information in both internal and external markets; (4) analyzing the material and data gathered; and (5) presenting the findings and results to management and the entire staff.

4. An analytical marketing system is typically conducted by outside consultants with a staff of statisticians who run the data through advanced statistical procedures and models based on similar studies and researches for comparison, analysis, and dissection.

Using the Web for Information Gathering

After you have completed the planning process with your team – reviewing existing market conditions, company brand, possible competitors, and the specific information you want to research – the World Wide Web provides another enormous source of information. The following is a list of some good places to start your web research. Keep in mind that given the ever-changing state of the Internet, the links on this list are bound to become outdated after publication.

Associations

Industry associations are often overlooked as a source of information, but they can furnish you with a variety of data to facilitate comprehensive market research. Most associations can provide calendars, back issues of publications, contacts for staff members, and information on current code and regulatory issues. Many have conducted research that may be of help to you and may have access to data that could be useful. Lastly, most associations have a help line that provides the opportunity to ask questions regarding particular issues.

- *American Council of Engineering Companies:* www.acec.org

- *American Institute of Architects:* www.aia.org

- *American Institute of Steel Construction:* www.aisc.org

- *American Marketing Association:* www.ama.org

- *American Public Works Association:* www.apwa.net

- *American Subcontractors Association:* www.asaonline.com/eweb

- *American Society for Healthcare Engineering:* www.ashe.org

- *American Society of Association Executives:* www.asaecenter.org

- *American Society of Civil Engineers:* www.asce.org

- *American Society of Concrete Contractors:* www.ascconline.org

- *American Society of Mechanical Engineers:* www.asme.org

- *American Society of Landscape Architects:* www.asla.org

- *American Wood Council:* www.awc.org

- *Associated Builders and Contractors:* www.abc.org

- *Associated General Contractors of America:* www.agc.org

- *Associated Owners & Developers:* www.constructionchannel.net

- *Association of Foreign Investment in Real Estate:* www.afire.org

- *ASTM International:* www.astm.org

- *Builders Owners and Managers Association International:* www.boma.org

- *Commercial Real Estate Development Association:* www.naiop.org

- *Construction Institute:* www.construction.org

- *Construction Management Association of America:* www.cmaanet.org

- *Construction Owners Association of America:* www.coaa.org

- *Construction Specifications Institute:* www.csinet.org

- *Construction Users Roundtable:* www.curt.org

- *Design-Build Institute of America:* www.dbia.org

- *Institute of Electrical and Electronics Engineers, Inc.:* www.ieee.org

- *International Council of Shopping Centers:* www.icsc.org

- *International Facility Management Association:* www.ifma.org

- *Lean Construction Institute:* www.leanconstruction.org

- *National Association of Home Builders:* www.nahb.com

- *National Association of Women in Construction:* www.nawic.org

- *National Institute of Building Sciences:* www.nibs.org

- *National Network of Commercial Real Estate Women:* www.crewnetwork.org

- *National Society of Professional Engineers:* www.nspe.org

- *Society of Industrial and Office Realtors:* www.sior.com

- *Society for Marketing Professional Services:* www.smps.org

- *The Infrastructure Security Partnership:* www.tisp.org

- *Urban Land Institute:* www.uli.org

- *Washington Building Congress:* www.wbcnet.org

Government Databases

Government databases can provide the statistics you may need regarding general economic trends, housing starts, construction-put-in-place, a new market territory, market size, or potential revenue sources.

- *FedBizOpps:* The single government point-of-entry for federal government procurement opportunities over $25,000 (www.fedbizopps.gov).

- *Federal Trade Commission:* Offers good links to other business-oriented websites (www.ftc.gov).

- *Fedmarket.com:* Online community for government buyers and vendors (www.fedmarket.com).

- *FedWorld:* Managed by the National Technical Information Service, this website is a gateway to government information (http://fedworld.ntis.gov).

- *House of Representatives:* (www.house.gov).

- *Library of Congress:* Online information on books about the building industry (www.loc.gov).

- *Occupational Safety and Health Administration:* (www.osha.gov).

- *Securities and Exchange Commission:* Includes access to the Edgar database, which contains the full text of reports that public companies are required to file with the SEC, including quarterly financial statements (www.sec.gov).

- *Small Business Administration:* (www.sba.gov),

- *THOMAS:* Official source of U.S. legislative information on the Internet (http://thomas.loc.gov).

- *U.S. Business Advisor:* Gateway to government resources for business. (www.business.usa.gov).

- *U.S. Census Bureau:* Supplies a large volume of statistical data regarding locations within the United States (www.census.gov).

- *ZIP Code Lookup:* ZIP+4 information, compliments of the U.S. Postal Service (www.usps.gov/ncsc/lookups/lookup_zip+4.html).

Publications

The following publications may be read online; some of them are free, while others require a subscription. This is only a small subset of the design and construction-relevant publications that you may access.

- *Architectural Record:* www.archrecord.construction.com

- *Bloomberg Businessweek:* www.bloomberg.com

- *Builder:* www.builderonline.com

- *Buildings:* www.buildings.com

- *Construction Executive:* www.constructionexec.com

- *Constructor:* www.constructormagazine.com

- *Contractor:* www.contractormag.com

- *Design Intelligence:* www.di.net

- *Engineering Inc.:* www.acec.org

- *Engineering News-Record:* www.enr.com

- *Integration Quarterly:* www.dbia.org/resource-center

- *Metropolis:* www.metropolismag.com

Resource Websites

Listed below are several industry websites that can provide background research material for your next marketing plan or budget.

- *Advertising Age:* Information on advertising and marketing, plus the latest in marketing news (www.adage.com).

- *Bizjournals:* Source for a number of local papers that focus on business news and development, including information on markets you may be considering moving into (www.bizjournals.com).

- *BusinessWire:* Information, primarily in the form of press releases, about American companies (www.businesswire.com).

- *CMD (formerly Reed Construction Data):* Includes numerous products, including Clark Reports, Daily Commercial News, First Source, and the RSMeans product line (www.cmdgroup.com).

- *Dun & Bradstreet (D&B):* A database of millions of U.S. businesses; offers tips on a variety of business-related topics and information on many public corporations, including background reports complete with sales figures, employee information, markets, and special promotional events (www.dnb.com).

- *Federal Contracts:* Information regarding companies doing business with the federal government (www.fedspending.org).

- *Hoover's Online:* A website that provides information about thousands of publicly-held and larger private companies (www.hoovers.com).

- *McGraw-Hill Construction:* Includes links to a wealth of construction information, including the company's Dodge and Sweets products and an online bookstore with more than 2,000 titles of books and software for the construction industry (www.construction.com).

- *Minority Business & Professional Directory:* Directory of businesses owned by minorities and women (www.minoritybusinessdir.com).

- *Online Resources for the Construction Industry:* Provides a free e-mail newsletter (www.copywriter.com/constr.htm)

- *PR Newswire:* Source of press releases for thousands of companies (www.prnewswire.com).

- *PSMJ Resources, Inc.:* Lists free offerings as well as marketing and consulting publications and seminars that are available for a fee (www.psmj.com).

- *ThomasRegister:* Online resource listing U.S. manufacturers, including information on millions of individual products, services, and companies (www.thomasnet.com).

- *US Companies:* Provides (local) public and private company profiles (www.manta.com).

Finally, you should consult the index of Sam Richter's book, *Take the Cold Out of Cold Calling: Web Search Secrets* (Adams Business & Professional, 2010), as well as his online newsletter, Warm Call Center (www.warmcallcenter.com). This is a powerful resource that provides numerous tips on using the web to access the information you need to understand your prospective clients and to beat your competition.

Do not be intimidated by the huge amount of resources before you. This chapter has listed some of the most useful databases and websites, and undoubtedly new resources will be developed even as this book is being published and distributed. Search engines will change and multiply, and applications (apps) will continue to offer new sources of information. Your task is to use these resources in a systematic and meaningful way. Remember our "three-legged stool" for marketing: Your objectives are to get a better handle on the unique services that your firm offers, the specific needs and challenges of your potential clients, and the strengths and weaknesses of your competitors. If you keep those goals in mind, the data will not feel so overwhelming. ■

Things to Think About

- How can my firm improve its market research strategies?

- Do our marketing strategies reflect a good understanding of who we are?

- Do we have a good grasp of our clients' needs?

- Do we have an accurate perception of our likely competitors?

- How can we use the web more effectively to gather market intelligence?

CHAPTER FIVE

Develop Your Marketing Strategy

Things You Will Learn From This Chapter

- Some different definitions of marketing.

- Why mission statements are important.

- How to develop a situational analysis.

- Key elements of a marketing plan.

- Basics of a go/no go decision.

AHALF CENTURY AGO, there was little said, written, or published about marketing. The A/E/C industry did not think of marketing as a necessary function; the perception of marketing was promotion-driven; an ad hoc, project-oriented effort. Firms did some modest advertising, printed a few brochures, and reluctantly made some cold calls. Long-term planning was unheard of, but since it was considered the leading-edge marketing effort for the industry, most business owners did not pursue it. Sales were the consuming activity. Estimating, pricing, and bidding was the common road map that firms followed in order to get business.

It was considered unprofessional, outrageous, or even unethical for service professionals such as attorneys, doctors, accountants, architects, engineers, and contractors to "market" themselves. For example, when a lawyer opened an office, he hung up his shingle, had his name listed in the local telephone book, and waited for business. The concept that marketing could apply to professional occupations was revolutionary and many shied away from it, but in time, there came a radical shift in the business world as professionals realized that they needed visibility and active promotion of their services in order for this business to succeed.

Passive and Silent No More

Suddenly, television and radio commercials were rife with professional advertising, and print ads were visible everywhere. There were shock waves. What were these lawyers and doctors thinking of? Was this ethical, moral, or in "good taste"? It was no longer considered "poor taste" to advertise your services, and that you were a skilled professional open for business.

The gurus of the business world jumped in and validated this new professional position. The concept was legitimized by Peter Drucker, the famous management expert and author of many books, including *The Effective Executive: The Definitive Guide to Getting the Right Things Done* (HarperBusiness, 2006), when he wrote that the sole purpose of business is to create customers, and that business has only two basic functions: marketing and innovation.

Jack Miller, a civil engineer from Houston, TX, who founded the Jack Miller Network (www.jackmiller.com), wrote about the importance of the marketing plan: "A company without a plan is like a ship without a rudder. It moves aimlessly in the marketplace reacting to pipe dreams instead of real opportunities." His belief was that once this plan was in place, you could then start making things happen.

Many design and construction firms still follow this concept. Too often, technically savvy companies have lost out to the firm that had superior marketing skills, because their executives knew what the market and its clients wanted. While these firms are still able to deliver services on time and within budget, their strength is their client relationships. Successful companies are not focused on being a "bid machine," but instead strive to focus their time and attention on a few quality client companies, and doggedly pursue them with high-quality service.

Had it ever occurred to you, when a particular product becomes the leader in its field, that it may not be better or worse than a similar product on the shelf, but has reached its position simply because of superior marketing? Perhaps this is true of all products. Is Budweiser a better beer, or are its executives better marketers? Does Pepsi and Coca-Cola taste exactly the same, or does the market leader taste better because it had a better marketing campaign? If this is true of all products, the same could be said of professional services. Have we had great experiences with products, or have we been brainwashed to believe one is better because one company's marketing campaign is more successful than the other?

Some Definitions of Marketing: Different Perspectives

Theodore Levitt, former editor of *Harvard Business Review* and author of *The Marketing Imagination* (Free Press, 1986), and other works, stresses that selling lets clients know what you have, whereas marketing strives to develop what the client wants at a price he is willing to pay.

Ben C. Gerwick, civil and environmental engineer and author of *Construction of Offshore Structures* (CRC Press, 2007), and other books, stated this premise in another way when he noted that marketing is an essential element in the survival and growth of design and construction organizations. He defines marketing as developing strong relationships that enable companies to sell its services in the most favorable places, and with the best terms and time frames.

Content marketing is the opposite of traditional advertising. It is based on supplying customers with critical information, often using a variety of media formats, without "shouting" explicit promotional messages. As Robert Rose, chief strategist at the Content Marketing Institute, slyly observed, "Traditional marketing and advertising is telling the world you're a rock star. Content marketing is showing the world that you are one."

In his book *Permission Marketing: Turning Strangers into Friends, and Friends into Customers* (Simon & Schuster, 1999), Seth Godin discusses how to build an ongoing relationship of increasing depth with your customers, particularly in a world muddled with many competing marketing messages. "Permission marketing" is a strategy in which a prospect explicitly agrees in advance to receive marketing content. As Godin puts it, this approach "turns strangers into friends, and friends into customers."

Randy Tuminello, author of the amusing (but also serious) *What You Need to Know about Doughnuts – And 35 More Marketing Success Stories* (SMPS, 2003), emphasizes the human factor in successful marketing pursuits. He sees marketing being most successful when technical competence and common courtesy meet. Tuminello notes that "when you consider what clients want most, your marketing messages will take on a completely different tone and emphasis."

Herman Holtz, author of numerous books on business and consulting, said, "Anyone can sell cold drinks to thirsty people. Marketing is the art of finding or inventing ways to make people thirsty." W. Chan Kim and Renée Mauborgne take this point further in *Blue Ocean Strategy: How to Create Uncontested Market Space and Make the Competition Irrelevant* (Harvard Business School Press, 2005). They note that on one level, some firms compete principally on price and function (rational appeal), while other firms compete mainly on feelings (emotional appeal). In fact, the appeal of most products or services is typically not one or the other, but rather a function of the way firms have competed in the marketplace, which has "unconsciously educated consumers what to expect."

These definitions reinforce the idea that marketing is a direct step to customer satisfaction and provides customers with the goods, products, or services they want. The result, when successful, could be a handsome profit, but it is not automatic. How many times have you been in a meeting when the discussion turns to pushing a service that your company wants to sell, but not necessarily what the market wants to buy? This is a common, universal dilemma, and it is a challenge that you, as a marketer, will constantly confront. Marketing today is a complex mix of traditional and digital marketing, as shown in *Figure 5.1* below.

Figure 5.1 *Marketing Mix.*

Marketing is based on two basic beliefs: (1) that your company policies, operations, and planning should be oriented toward the customer; and (2) that profitable sales volume should be the ultimate end result of the marketing plan. Thus, marketers are finding methods to satisfy client expectations so they can receive reasonable profits. The definition of marketing has evolved into a total company philosophy that integrates and coordinates all marketing activities within all company operations for the fundamental purpose of maximizing the bottom line for the firm. This is not an option; it is a mandate for any company whose owners want to be successful. How many company presidents believe that marketing is a simple process in which you hire a marketing director, and watch contracts and money roll in? It rarely works that way.

Marketing is a much more extensive framework of resources and tools. Most new marketing directors take a year to get anything accomplished because it takes at least that long for their marketing plan to gain a foothold. Also, new marketing managers need more tools and resources than a simple company credit card to be truly effective. Everyone in the organization must be committed to being a part of this marketing process and support it. Regular meetings should be held to discuss the company's goals and to sum up results of the marketing effort. Additional marketing content should be developed as an integral part of the marketing process. Direct marketing, a social media presence, the traditional company brochure, special marketing events, public relations activities, and industry involvement are all a part of this process.

If implemented properly, this process—a plan, a team, complete backup, marketing materials—can increase your market share by 30 to 50 percent. But before you jump right into marketing, you must plan. This is one step that almost everyone feels is inessential, but ignoring this process can result in chaos, confusion, and a dead end. The plan must lay out what you need to do, when you need to do it, and how the top executives and the entire staff will back up the person responsible for managing the marketing plan before they go into battle.

Achieving What You Want through Mission Statements

The first step in the planning process is the establishment of a mission statement. Just what do you want to accomplish? And where do you begin?

Scott Butcher, Vice President and Director of Business Development for JDB Engineering, Inc. and affiliate companies, described the purpose of the mission statement clearly when he said, "The mission statement is your destination. The marketing plan, in conjunction with the strategic plan, is your road map to get there."

This is echoed by Richard Sides, construction specialist and consultant with Strategies That Work, Grapevine, TX, who believes the corporate mission statement is the most important segment of your marketing plan because it clarifies your company's primary priority—to attract and keep customers.

The mission statement is the guiding light that directs your efforts. It also illustrates that everyone in the organization, not just the marketing team, is part of the solution and helps to impress on everyone that a team approach to marketing, and attention to satisfying the customer must be on everyone's mind.

Marketing Mix

The concept of the marketing mix has become the base from which marketing is developed within any company. The mix of activities that mesh the customer's wants and needs with other external environmental factors will create a successful marketing program. It is this diagnosis that determines where your business is positioned compared to the rest of the industry. Step back and take the time to examine this factor so that you are not blindsided to the perceptions that exist about your firm, and its position in the industry. Remember, it does not matter what you think about your company; it is important what your potential clients think about your firm.

As you build your program and examine your marketing mix, keep this priority uppermost in your mind. Your chance for success will become much higher with this approach. It is simple, straightforward, and by far the most logical sequence for your marketing and sales effort. An existing service to an existing client who is satisfied and happy with your past relationship will always provide your firm the greatest financial reward.

Situational Analysis

A situational analysis is one of the first steps you must take before beginning to assemble your marketing plan. The situational analysis consists of simply looking at your current competitive environment, getting a clear view of where the company can grow, and learning what services, perceptions, resources, and clients your competition uses. You should compare this analysis to your own functions to see where the differences are. Are you a market leader, a challenger, a follower, or a niche player? The analysis should include a discussion of prices, differentiation, barriers to entry to your desired segment of the business, and the unique advantages you may have. What trends have come and gone? What segments of the market are thriving, and why? Which segments are doing poorly? The analysis can be as complex and extensive as you need, but generally a more compact and precise overview will give you a better understanding of what has transpired during the past year.

Regular, up-to-date information regarding each competitor should be maintained in your firm's database. This should include photographs of your competitors' work, and what your competitors' clients are saying about them. As we noted in Chapter 4, you cannot effectively pursue new markets or new clients in a vacuum; it has to be within the context of your competitive environment. One of the greatest errors a firm can make, according to C. F. Culler Associates of Atlanta, is "overlooking the importance of this type of analysis, using general descriptions, and omitting market research that supports demand."

You may at some point have hired a consultant to do a situational analysis for you and may have received a hefty report that landed somewhere on a shelf, without it really being examined or read by anyone. If that is so, this is the time to take it out and read it. No matter how old it may be, summarize it in a few paragraphs, and see to it that the entire team reads that summary. What have you learned? Does any of this material apply to your current situation? Has there been radical changes in the structure of your organization and in its outlook? If you find anything of value in the old analysis, could it be a launching pad for a new one? Or can it serve as an outline? It is always wise to make use of all existing information.

Whether or not you have an existing analysis, you know that you need new information. Now is the time for a group analysis of where you are and where you are going. A thorough discussion of all segments of your business should be conducted with your office staff, clients, industry groups, and associations. The results of these discussions, along with a review and summary of the data uncovered in your initial research efforts, will paint a clearer picture of what has transpired in the past year. An in-depth analysis of the strengths and weaknesses of the company is paramount.

Here are some questions and issues you should address:

- What type of business are you in now, and where do you want to be in five to ten years?

- What is your current sales volume?

- What are your current profit goals, and are you making them consistently?

- What are your company's strengths?

- What are your company's weaknesses?

- What would you like to add to your scope of services and/or products?

- What type of potential clients are you looking for?

- What is your preferred way of doing business?

- What are your company goals now, and how have you reached them in the past?

- What assets and resources do you have with regard to people, equipment, and technical capabilities?

- What trends do you foresee within your internal and external market?

- Are you willing to expand geographically?

These questions can be organized in the form of a SWOT analysis that the entire organization can build around. This analysis systematically reviews all major internal and external environmental conditions that may affect your organization. Ideally, this inventory of your market should be conducted off-site in a retreat setting, where the entire staff can brainstorm and offer their own ideas and beliefs. The team should also update this inventory at least once a year.

Market segmentation will follow the development of a company SWOT analysis; this is a placement of customers within grids based on the strengths defined. Market segmentation enables marketers to focus their time and effort on a targeted market group. This segmentation should illustrate a diverse group of client types that can be further analyzed based on profitability. An example of how this information may be laid out is shown in *Figure 5.4 (p. 95).*

This table can be expanded to include the total market share, as well as what your percentage of each share is and where you believe it could be. The ultimate purpose of this process is to find

Component	Description
Table of Contents	Listing of plan components.
Executive Summary	Management summary of entire plan.
Company strategic mission	Vision, Goals, and strategies of company.
SWOT analysis	Research and data analysis of internal and external market conditions garnered from media, private industry, government, associations, etc.
	Market forecasts/market share/trend assessment. Company resources (people, equipment, funding)
Marketing Mix	Development of four Ps: product, price, promotion, place.
	Life cycle service/product strategies, previous sales history and future projections, client, prospects.
	Pricing issues. Promotional activities (marketing communications).
	Place-distribution challenges within market and target markets.
Strategic Plan	Putting the above elements together for a cohesive plan, reviewing current resources for supplementing plan, developing a budget and tentative time frame.
Action Plans	Goals and task assignment to achieve plan. Who, what, when, where, and how, with costs and schedule to be monitored.
Controls and review	Regular reviews to update and adjust marketing plan.

Figure 5.2 *Marketing Plan Components.*

homogeneous groupings of potential prospects whose requirements are essentially the same, so that you can target your marketing approach.

A review of the marketing life cycle is also an important step when making any decision at this stage of the planning process. Products and services are thought of as having a life that begins with their introduction, continues through the growth and maturity stages, and ends in decline. The potential life cycle of any product or service is important to keep in mind as your analysis takes shape. Initially, there is minimal competition when a new product or service is introduced, and the volume and profits of the introduction shows a curve that starts an upward incline. As the service or product goes into the growth phase, the curve moves upward. As the service or product reaches the mature state, inevitably there is a gradual, and then a more severe, decline. This is normal for any product. Needless to say, as you analyze your position with a situational analysis, you want to attempt to position yourself as close to the introduction of any new service or product's life cycle as possible. This ensures a moderate guarantee of a significant volume of business opportunities, and the opportunity to maximize your profit potential.

When you view the marketing strategies of companies that sell products, you can see what they do with their life cycles. Observe the fast food industry, for instance. A new hamburger is introduced and is marketed heavily. It reaches a peak as long as it stands alone. As soon as the competition gets in, the first hamburger reaches a plateau and begins to decline. Management introduces a new wrinkle, or a new product, or several new products in succession, or a new way of presenting the same old hamburger. View any product or service company in the world, and you will see the same life cycle. To reach that high peak is an achievement. To keep it takes ingenuity, creativity, and imagination.

Strategies + Action Plans = Marketing Plan

The marketing plan is your road map to success in charting a five-year plan of action for your firm. Without a plan, you can get off course and waste considerable time, money, and resources. Most companies cannot afford not to plan in today's business arena. According to Frank Stasiowski, founder of PSMJ/Resources in Newton, MA, and lecturer, author/publisher of a number of business books, there are five elements necessary for a successful marketing strategy: (1) analyzing the marketplace; (2) researching the client; (3) understanding how your firm is perceived by clients; (4) investigating the competition; and (5) conducting an internal assessment.

Stasiowski goes on to state that these five elements are common to all Fortune 500 companies. The strategic marketing planning process provides the total framework for a contractor or design firm. With this process, principals can gain a clear direction toward the vision, and mission of the firm, the steps necessary to reach their goals, the objectives established, and a clear road map for the entire team within the organization.

Planning is critical and can help define your goals for the coming year. It should include the structure, timetable, resources needed, and an action plan for the staff, with assignments for each. Without a plan, the marketing effort can wander aimlessly with much less productivity than it would have otherwise. Develop your own plan with all your strategic planning tools; this will drive your firm toward the opportunities that await, and you will avoid pitfalls. Where you choose to focus your efforts and your management philosophy will dictate how you should guide and train your staff. Keep in mind the following key aspects of this "risk versus opportunity" aspect of your plan.

You cannot always eliminate all risk, because any business is a gamble, and all businesses incur risks. However, the following ideas may help you to reduce some of the risk:

- Look out for threats.

- Reduce self-performed work (outsource more non-essential activities).

- Schedule what needs to be accomplished during the year.

- Administer contracts diligently.

- React aggressively to internal and external threats.

To enhance opportunities:

- Look internally for opportunities within your organization.

- Increase internal performance of activities that are your specialty.

- Plan to complete the work by an established schedule.

- Manage your plan around completed work goals (results), building your record and reputation.

The marketing plan should be your proactive approach to business. You should strive to think outside the box, anticipating the risks you may face and the opportunities on which you may be able to capitalize. You are not marketing the quarter-inch drill bit, but rather the quarter-inch hole; this analogy should be the underlying theme that permeates your game plan. The plan must incorporate all available information about your firm, your advantages and disadvantages, and the strategy and reputation of your competitors.

Function	Activity	Responsibility	Due Date	Done
SWOT analysis	Research	rdw	12/1/2015	
Marketing mix development	Four P's analysis			
Strategic plan development	Assemble cohesive elements			
Action plans (to accomplish strategic plan)	Goal 1 Goal 2 Goal 3			
Controls	Review of plan activities			

Figure 5.3 *Marketing Plan Strategies.*

Figure 5.2 (p. 85) is a basic outline of a marketing plan and its different components. Every plan will have at least a summary, a SWOT, specific goals and objectives, strategies, and an action plan.

Having a summary with conclusions is self-evident, and yet many firms fail to put their full report into a readable summary that can be utilized to focus their efforts throughout the year. The summary should reinforce your mission statement and provide background material.

Investors and top management may not read much further than the executive summary, making this document even more critical to guaranteeing the financial support you will need to implement your full plan. If you are using outside financing to push your projects forward, bank officials will want to see your plan; in addition, expect to provide them your financial statements, balance sheets, bank statements, tax returns, internal bookkeeping records, and more. But you can present all of your financial information and still be rejected unless you present a succinct business plan and marketing plan. Consider your marketing plan and situational analysis not only as a working guideline, but also as a financial instrument.

Previously we examined the various components of research. This is one particular segment of the plan that needs sufficient time and attention to allow you to fully grasp the depth of the industry, its players, and the trends that will shape its future. You will need time to review the information you have obtained from industry publications, newspapers, magazines, newsletters, online sources, associations, government agencies, and private industry groups. All of these are excellent sources for viable business information; you should not neglect any of these, particularly industry reports.

Goals and objectives provide the basis for what the company hopes to achieve from the marketing plan. This is really the meat and potatoes of the plan, which can be broken into various sub-plans for the firm's future. Management is tuned-in to the sales plan you intend to influence through this marketing agenda, but there are several areas that will be affected by your advertising, marketing research, marketing collateral, training, technology, and public relations plans. It is best that the goals and objectives set be as specific and measurable as possible.

Strategies and tactics are the procedures used by the company's marketing department to achieve the goals of the plan. What specific agenda will the company establish in order to achieve this plan?

Recommended actions (the action plan) are the heart of the plan. This is where the principals provide specific actions and outline the tasks to be performed, who will perform them, and when and how they will be performed.

Typical Marketing Plan

Let us now create a sample marketing plan. Remember that mission statements do not limit your freedom of choice in deciding where you are and where you plan to go. In many ways, they free you from having to consistently analyze the strategic decisions your company must face. Knowing what your business is, who your clients are, and what each of your clients' values give you and your team so you can obtain a clear direction should resonate with the firm's mission statement, goals and objectives.

Create a list as follows:

1. Existing clients.

2. Future clients.

3. Market areas in which we currently work and those we want to expand into.

4. Products and/or services we provide.

5. What are our financial objectives?

6. What skill do we particularly excel at?

7. What are the company's core values and beliefs?

8. What do we want to achieve for the employees of the company?

9. What image do we want to have established in the marketplace 10 years from now?

10. Mission statement.

Market size

You have unlimited access to statistical data regarding the market area. Forecasting the total size of your potential market, while also breaking it into specific segments (i.e., retail, commercial, government, private, etc.) should not be difficult; however, it will take some time, and will require considerable analysis to make sure the information you have located is correct and meets your needs. This research should be used throughout your marketing plan to help you make decisions about resource allocations in the pursuit of new business development. You should never depend entirely on what you uncover on the Internet or from print media. Go out and talk with leaders in the market you want to enter, and network with potential clients. Talk with contractors, developers, owners, and economic development agencies to learn their thoughts. You can also supplement this process with telephone interviews, and perhaps even some mail surveys. During your planning meetings, you will be able to quote their view of the future rather than your own, which will reinforce your thinking and build buy-in from your planning team. The following questions may help you develop information about your market.

- What is the size of the market in land volume and dollars?

- What is the size of various market segments in land volume and dollars?

- How established (old) is this market?

- Is the market receptive to price fluctuation?

- Is the market receptive to outside fluctuations?

- Is this market cyclical? If so, can you determine the patterns and their cyclical sequences?

- How difficult is it to wrest market share away from the current industry leaders? Are there opportunities to penetrate this market despite the current dominant leaders in the (construction or other) industry?

- What unique skills, attitudes, and technologies are involved in the market?

This kind of planning is suitable for any service provider, but certainly more so for architects, engineers, construction workers, landscape designer, or any design professional.

Strengths and Weaknesses

Earlier we reviewed the benefits of a SWOT analysis for your firm and your market. This is a critical stage of the planning process when developing a situational analysis of your firm's strengths, goals, opportunities, weaknesses, and assets.

This same review of competitors, using a SWOT analysis, will allow you to gather important information regarding each of them. For example, one subcontractor has developed a competitor analysis sheet that reviews the results of each project it bids, documenting the bid results, the winner, the winner's bid, the winner's margin (against the contractor's own estimate), the winner's backlog, whether pre-construction services were provided, the number and names of competitors, the contractor's backlog at the time of bid, the customer relationship, and the anticipated start and end dates of the project.

This document also lists all the key project players, including the owner/developer, architect, engineer, and construction manager with an address, contact, and phone number for each. The project is described in depth with the building type, size based on gross square feet, the floors, what the structural system is, an arbitrary rating of the complexity of the project, and the delivery system. Added to this is an analysis of the design data: typical bay sizes, super live and dead loads, typical story height, seismic zone, lateral system, and other technological features the structure may contain. The firm is then in a position to monitor the preferences, backlog, relationships, and intricacy of its competitor base and to control its pricing and market planning. Your analysis may not go to this extent, but remember, your competitor has the same tools available as you so it is best to try to obtain a good description of your strengths and weaknesses and those of your competitor as soon as you can.

Where Are We Today? Where Do We Want to Be Tomorrow?

Many companies are so busy doing current work, executing projects, putting out fires, and looking for new business opportunities that they neglect to look toward the future. It is hard to think about the day after tomorrow when you're so busy today that you can scarcely keep up. However, forecasting five years into the future, with key employees to help, is an essential activity. During one of your early morning planning sessions, spend a bit of time writing a description of where you want the firm to be five years from now. Be as detailed as possible. What markets are you in, how many employees do you have, what market segments are you participating in, how are you perceived in the market, and how do your employees feel about the organization? This document then becomes the road map to your firm's future.

The next part of the marketing plan will provide the objectives and actions to be taken to get the company to this destination.

Identifying Prospects

Another important step of any marketing plan is determining who needs your services. Start with developing a list of who has been buying your services or products over the last five years. Break down this list of names into the market segments in which they participate. Examples could be commercial owners, government agencies, owner representatives, and the like. Then start to list the volume of work you have obtained from each. Some clients demand an excessive amount of time with little or no payback in the form of new business. There is a tendency to develop a comfort level with these clients because we talk with them regularly, providing pricing and assisting with information requests. But they're tire-kickers; they have no intention of buying, just picking your brain for information. Some of these clients can take up an inordinate amount of your time without adding significantly to your balance sheet. Get rid of them! You are too busy to be hand-holding!

The final step of this stage is to pinpoint your project locations. The next stage involves developing a list of potential clients. Who are the people with whom you'd like to do business? Have you thought of new segments of the market, new territories, and clients with a good reputation for professionalism, fast payment of invoices, and low maintenance during the execution of the project? During your initial research, were there industry names that surfaced repeatedly?

Summarize your existing clients and the locations where you have performed their work. You need to examine your actual results, and strive to provide realistic guidance as to where you have had profitable results and where you have done a great deal of work but with marginal profits.

One of the most difficult aspects of this industry is eliminating opportunities that exist but does not provide profit. Unless you have committed yourself to good causes, pro bono work, doing people favors, or taking on jobs that do not allow you to cover salaries, you need to think twice before taking on a project at cost. There is some justification to maintaining this type of backlog of work if it helps eliminate or absorb some of your fixed costs and overhead. However, many firms have been coerced into believing that a large backlog is the panacea for all of their problems when in most cases, it only adds to the stress. Remember the 80/20 rule: 80 percent of your profits usually come from 20 percent of your clients. Managing the 80 percent is critical to your overall success.

During this activity, it is also important to analyze client needs as best you can. Basic to such a review is how each client has rated each of the following aspects of your business: price, quality, service, location or convenience to his company's office, financial background, the training within your company, how your style or image meshes with his company's needs, exclusivity, product/service line, availability, warranty for services provided, ease to work with (evidenced by minimal change-orders and back charges), knowledge of the market, reliability, and on-time delivery of the project as contracted. Being able to satisfy each specific client need is the difference between a contract and no contract. Price is important, but there are many important variables in the final decision.

Image

Here is the portion of the mission statement that should set the standard for all of your actions. What image do you want to give the marketplace, your clients, potential clients, and the A/E/C community in general? Marketing, as you will recall, is in large part a matter of perception. Based on your research, what is the external perception of your firm? What perception do you want people to have about you?

All firms today stress quality, within-budget, on-time performance. With that as the basic requirement, what does your company have to offer? This is the time to consider any niche opportunities you may have, your company's special market segmentation aspects, and any special strengths. The James G. Davis Construction Company in Rockville, MD specializes in suburban office buildings and advertises this specialty widely. The company conveys the idea that it is the building owner's "personal contractor" and goes out of its way to provide an environment that is a positive experience for the building owner. This philosophy and effort permeates all levels of the organization, from the secretary to the field forces. Whom do you think owners and their friends turn to first when they have another project to negotiate? Certainly someone who conveys that he cares about the project, takes a personal interest, and thus earns good marks from all his clients. "Oh, yes, we use Jim Davis exclusively. He takes care of our needs personally."

Qualifying Prospects – Your Go/No Go Process

There are hundreds of prospective customers in your markets, and it is your job to determine the few who will provide you with the best opportunities. Deciding what is important and who is worthy of your firm's time and attention will pay real dividends. The following questions explore the types of issues that you should consider before pursuing a particular client. Creating a go/no go process at the strategic level can help you when making day-to-day decisions. Here are some things to consider when creating your process:

1.   *Is this project real?* You can burn a lot of energy, time, and emotion on projects that are little more than pie-in-the-sky. Make sure the project has actually been scheduled and funded, and verify who is behind it. Do not let someone who has a reputation for fantasizing sell you on committing to a project when he has not yet talked to a bank, nailed down the specifics, signed all the paperwork, and set up all the participants.

2.   *Does this project fit into your company's mission and purpose?* This new project or client may seem exotic and have many good attributes, but if it does not meet the marketing mix you have established with your team members, then it should be shelved for the time being. However, if you do not have a schedule of upcoming business to keep your people busy and you need to keep them working, then you can, and probably should, consider an offbeat project, provided that your team is experienced enough to do it properly.

3. *Where is the project located?* If this potential project falls outside of your current territory, it may require an unusual amount of resources to oversee its execution, and it may impose new risks.

4. *Who is the competition?* A review of who will be your anticipated competitors is important. Do any of your competitors have a personal relationship with the buying authority on this project? If it is a very close relationship, the project may be considered "wired," meaning another firm is already slated to win the project.

5. *Will it be hard-bid or negotiated?* Will you have fifteen competitors or three? Will it be first cost or best final?

6. *Who will be the design team?* Some designers have a reputation for flair but lack the ability to assemble executable working documents. Will you be assuming additional risks?

7. *How will it be financed?* Will the financing be through bond issues, banks, or insurance companies? If you are to be a part of this project, you must know what the financial commitment and risks will be. If the project is not solidly financed, there is a chance you will not be paid.

8. *How big is the project?* Sometimes a project should be disqualified immediately due to its size, whether it is too large or too small. If the project is too large for your particular resources, consider joint-venturing.

Deciding to go after a specific project should not be based on a whim or gut feeling. You should develop a rigorous process to make the decision to pursue a project (go/no go) as objective as possible. You have limited marketing resources so you should only use them to try to win projects that are in accord with the long-term objectives of your marketing plan.

Action Plans That Generate Strategies for Follow-up

Now that you have defined the markets in which you want to work and grow, have identified potential clients that have a profitable record, the most important stage of your marketing plan is the establishment of your action plans. Planning is important, but every human endeavor needs a push to get it moving. Start with an overall strategy for translating your marketing plan into an action plan. For business development-related strategies, action plans can include capture plans. Break the guiding plan into manageable pieces with competitive and promotional strategies, including timetables for each, and assign an individual to be responsible for the marketing plan (see *Figure 5.3, p. 87*).

This is the step that will make or break most marketing plans. A regular review of the status of your marketing strategies, with critical discussions of your successes and failures, will assist with the redirection of your efforts. Accountability of individuals who are given responsibility is critical; these individuals will want to break down the action plan even further into manageable pieces. For example, if one of your strategies is to develop five new clients in the coming year, a subset of your plan will break down this objective as follows:

■ Meet with x, y, z potential clients in January

- Send letter of introduction with annual report, project profiles, etc.

- Follow-up call to be made one week later.

- Follow-up visit within two weeks.

- Obtain at least one new project from your initial effort.

- Meet with a, b, c potential clients in February.

- Continue the same sequence as January.

No plan works flawlessly. Every plan will need some modification because of unforeseen market conditions. But having a plan of action with a set timetable and accountable individuals will help your firm meet its financial goals.

Persuasion, Closing, and Getting the Project

Satisfying a client's need and persuading that client that your proposal should be accepted is an art form in itself. Why should the client do business with you? Make a conscious effort to prepare a list of benefits that you will bring to the table when you meet with your client and discuss it thoroughly in advance with your entire team. Are you being selected on the basis of quality, speed, scheduling, financial strength, a friendly and competent staff, no "nickel and diming" during or after the construction process, value-engineering talent, or an ability to consistently bring the project in under-budget? An enormous amount of time and effort is expended to get to this stage. Having made such a huge investment, you now want to ensure that you will close the sale.

Encouraging your clients to close now is of paramount importance. Consistently probe the client for additional information. Establish the kind of rapport that will make it easy for him or her to tell you what you need to know. If you sense there are hidden agendas, hesitation for any reason whatsoever, or something the prospective client is not telling you, it is up to you to find out. Ask questions:

- How much do you want to pay?

- When do you want to start the project?

- We have two ways we can proceed. Which one would you prefer?

At the same time, you can add subtle items within your discussion that are integral to your proposal, and that can trigger a need to close the deal. Perhaps you can add escalation terms to your proposal so your price will be increased or may not be applicable by a certain date. Create a verbal image of how the client will benefit when they sign on with you. Remind the client that time and profit will be lost by not acting in a timely manner. However, you cannot press too hard because then the client could become uneasy, and feel that you are the one with a hidden agenda. You need to proceed thoughtfully and carefully.

There is nothing illegal or unethical about these approaches. They are simply steps to move a project from dead center to a line of action that your client will have to make eventually. There are some people who cannot negotiate decisively. If your prospective client is one of these, you need to use your talent for persuasion to move them along. Your ability to get a final decision on projects can work for the benefit of everyone involved.

Monitoring and Making Changes

Now that you have completed your plan, and individuals have been given their assignments for tasks to be accomplished, it is time to implement a series of checks and balances to monitor the plan and to ensure that you have the flexibility to make changes if you encounter roadblocks. Contingency plans can be installed for "what if" scenarios based on resource and people problems. Schedules can be adjusted and regular feedback and discussions can connect activities that have led your efforts in a direction contrary to where you wanted to go.

A marketing plan is just that—a plan. It is a dynamic tool rather than a document that is tossed on a dusty shelf. It must be regularly reviewed, analyzed, changed, and modified. As with any road map you will encounter detours along the way, so your road map should be flexible. With the business world changing (sometimes overnight), the traditional five-year plan can be an albatross. So you should create a three-year plan to ensure that all departments in your organization are on the same page. Each division of the firm needs to provide feedback, allowing marketers to add their comments about budgeting modifications, human resource allocations, outside vendor assignments, and missed opportunities. Each time the marketing plan is reviewed or discussed, obstacles can be discussed and alternative solutions proposed.

The importance of investing in marketing activities cannot be stressed too much. This is an outlay of financial and human resources that needs consistent reassessment in the never-ending cycle of marketing. Controlling and accurately assessing the activities generated by the marketing plan are difficult and complex, but to be truly successful, they must be measured and monitored regularly. This effort will not be in vain. It will generate increased financial returns, general goodwill and enhanced motivation for everyone.

Monitoring methods can be both qualitative and quantitative. A review of the strategic action plan with anticipated results, compared to the overall operating statement of the company, needs to be made and discussed. The marketing plan should be aligned with the financial objectives of the organization (sales, growth, return on investment, etc.) and should be tied in with the compensation for the marketing staff.

Now It's Time to Do It

Take a look at Chris Baréz-Brown's *How to Have Kick-Ass Ideas: Shake Up Your Business, Shake Up Your Life.* (Skyhorse Publishing, 2008), a fun motivational book that will give you the courage and enthusiasm to "shake up your business, shake up your life" before you embark on your marketing plan. There will be so many obstacles once you start down this road that it is helpful to read about them beforehand and develop confidence that you can overcome them.

Marketing is an essential component of any A/E/C firm, and the marketing plan and how you implement it is critical to your firm's overall success. In order to develop commitment to the plan, you must communicate it with passion. Executives who neglect this essential component eventually will see their companies decline. As Peter Drucker once said, a plan is nothing "unless it generates work." ∎

Client Type	Less than $1 million	$1-5 million	$5-10 million	Larger than $10 million
Institutional				
Commercial				
Design-build				
Lump sum				
Negotiated				
Interior				
Full Construction				
Joint Ventures				

Figure 5.4 *Market Segmentation Grid.*

Things to Think About

- Does our firm's mission statement reflect who we are and where we want to go?

- Does our firm conduct an accurate situational analysis?

- Do we regularly review and update our marketing plan?

- Do we integrate recent market research into our marketing plan?

- Is our firm's go/no go strategy realistic?

CHAPTER SIX

Creating Your Marketing
Communications Plan

Things You Will Learn From This Chapter

- Why a marketing communication plan is the foundation of all of your promotional efforts.

- How establishing measurable goals and objectives will enable you to determine the effectiveness of your promotional efforts.

- The definition of the target audience as the people most likely to buy your products or services.

- Why you should narrow your audience down and speak to one person at a time for best results.

- How communicating the benefits rather than the features of your products or services will allow your target audiences to understand why they should buy from you.

- How to use the creative brief as a guide that takes you from where you are to where you want to be.

AMARKETING COMMUNICATION PLAN is an essential part of your marketing program that cannot be overlooked. This document can help you to identify what characteristics of your firm will appeal to a prospective client. It enables you to get to know your target audience in great detail, and it identifies which marketing channels are best suited to reach your prospects and which best fit your budget. Then it can help you find the best strategy for developing marketing programs that will drive your competitive advantages home in a way that will encourage prospective clients to take action.

The marketing communication plan will also help you establish measurable goals. You will be able to define, in concrete dollars-and-cents terms, whether or not your marketing communication program is working. Moreover, it will help you establish consistency in all of your marketing efforts. Once you determine what messages you must communicate and to whom, you can make sure that all of your marketing efforts will work in concert with one another to generate the results you want.

What Is Marketing Communication?

Simply put, marketing communication consists of communication efforts designed to support marketing goals.

Marketing communication puts the two activities – marketing and communicating – together. Marketing communication materials include anything you produce that communicates your marketing goals and objectives, such as your branding, website, direct marketing, advertising, and so on. Other marketing communication efforts such as publicity, helps get the word out about your services through the media, such as newspapers, websites, magazines, and newsletters.

Understanding marketing communications will help you identify outside resources that will best serve your needs. There are a number of marketing consultants, including sales trainers who can help you in this area. Likewise, there are advertising agencies whose primary function is to write, design, and place advertisements; and public relations firms that produce and place stories in the media, and stage events for publicity. There are also web developers, graphic designers, copywriters, SEO firms, and specialists of all kinds who are trained and experienced in the art of getting your message across to the outside world.

Companies that position themselves as marketing communication specialists typically provide a full range of services. They often integrate several marketing communication functions—web development, email marketing, advertising, and publicity—provide a complete package of marketing support.

Establishing Your Goals and Objectives

Before you decide whether or not you should build a website or develop a direct marketing campaign, you must establish your goals and objectives. Goals, in this case, are marketing goals that you should have determined when you developed your business and marketing plans. They define where you want to be in a given time period. The following are some examples of marketing goals:

- Enter a new geographic area and generate $1 million in fees in the coming 24 months.

- Introduce a new product or service to the marketplace in the coming year.

- Increase market share by five percent more than the past year.

- Generate a 50/50 mix of bid and negotiated work within the next two years.

- Become known as an expert in your field with the next 15 months.

From these goals, you should establish clear-cut communication objectives, the responses you desire from your target audience. You should develop as many communication objectives as possible for each of your marketing goals. For instance, if entering a new geographic area and generating $1 million in fees within the next 24 months is your goal, the following communication objectives could be established for you:

- Create awareness of your company.

- Create awareness of your product or services.

- Establish the need for your product or services.

- Communicate the benefits of your product or services.

- Establish a liking or preference for your product or services.

- Generate inquiries.

You will notice that each of these communication objectives work together to take the prospective buyer through the decision-making process: awareness, need, liking, and purchase. It is essential that you take a prospect through each step of this process.

In addition to helping you decide what you must do to accomplish your goals, communication objectives help you measure your results, determine how well you have accomplished each objective, and decide whether the money you spent on marketing generated the results you expected. Your objectives will help you isolate which parts of your marketing communication plan are working and which are not.

Measuring results is not as easy as determining whether or not your goals have been met. If your goal was to enter a new market, and generate $1 million in revenue within 24 months and you failed to do so, it is not necessarily the fault of your marketing communication plan. Variables not controlled by the marketing communication plan, such as price, quality, your salespeople's ability, and general economic conditions, may all contribute to your results. There may be market conditions, national crises, or international events you could not possibly have factored into your plan that can have an effect in everyone's business.

What you can measure is whether you have met your communication objectives. Have you established awareness? Have you established liking or preference? To measure how well you create awareness of your company or your competitive advantages, you might conduct a random survey of prospective clients before the marketing communication campaign begins and measure the percentage of your target audience that is aware of your company. After your campaign, you should conduct another random survey of a similar number of prospective clients to measure the percentage that is aware of your company and its services or products. Surveys could also measure whether your campaign has established liking or preference for your product or service. And, of course, if your objective is to generate responses, you can easily determine the number of responses in a given time period before and after your campaign.

Identifying Your Competitive Advantages

Every company that is at least modestly successful must have competitive advantages, characteristics that make it better than or different from those of the competition. If you think you are just like any other company, providing similar services, think again. You would not be in business if there were not something about your company that makes it different from the competition. Perhaps it is quality, or maybe price. Perhaps you have a technological edge, or maybe you are well-connected.

Regardless, it is imperative that you identify your competitive advantages because once you do, you need to communicate to them consistently in all your marketing efforts. Start by gathering a group of key people in your company (preferably those who have worked at the firm for a long time), interact often with clients, and have a good understanding of how you sell your products or services. Set aside enough time to talk without interruption. Use a white board or some other way for all participants to see what you are writing; create two columns. At the top of the left column, write "Competitive Advantages." Then brainstorm. Make a long list of all the characteristics that you feel are your company's strengths. They do not need to be unique to your company, and they do not necessarily need to be tasks you do better than every other company; they just need to be areas in which you feel your company particularly excels. This list could be as long as you feel is necessary to identity all the characteristics, either individually or collectively, that set you apart.

Figure 6.1 below shows a list of competitive advantages that a hypothetical interior architectural firm may identify.

Competitive Advantages of a
Hypothetical Interior Architectural Firm

1. We have been in business over 30 years.

2. Our people have significant experience in interior architecture, for both new construction and renovation.

3. We are innovators.

4. We are good listeners.

5. We have a flat organizational chart.

6. We have a lot of people with ownership in our company.

7. We are extremely service-oriented.

8. We are committed to quality.

9. We are nice people to work with.

10. We are community-minded.

Figure 6.1 *Competitive Advantages of a Hypothetical Interior Architectural Firm.*

Once you have identified your competitive advantages, you must translate them into their benefit to your clients. This is essential because people buy the benefits they derive from a product or service, not the features of the product or service (see *Figure 6.2, p. 103*). People do not use aspirin, for instance, because of its features: white, chalky, bitter-tasting, dry, and round. People use aspirin because of the benefit they receive from using it–pain relief. Similarly, people do not buy an air conditioner because it is a large, clunky, metal box with fans, pipes, and coils. They buy cool air.

Your services are no different. Yet all too often, companies, particularly in the A/E/C industry, promote the features of their products or services rather than the benefits to be derived from them. How often have you seen marketing materials that promote details like the experience of senior staff, experience designing similar projects, pre-construction services, or engineering expertise? These may indeed be competitive advantages, but they are communicated in terms of features rather than benefits. However, people buy the benefits they will receive from these competitive advantages.

The best way to identify the benefits of each of your competitive advantages is to submit it to the "So what?" test. For each advantage–experience, quality, and so forth–ask the question, "So what?" When the question is answered, again ask, "So what?" and keep asking it. When you can no longer answer the "So what?" question, you have identified the real benefit. Here is an example of how it works.

If your competitive advantage is "We have experience designing similar projects," (a feature), ask, "So what?"

You might answer, "Well, that means we are familiar with issues that might come up during construction."

Features Versus Benefits:
Wooden Stick or Writing Tool?

Here's a great way to hone your skills in identifying features instead of benefits. Remember that your features describe a product or services, while benefits describe the reward people get from using your product or service.

After you have gathered your key staff and identified your company's competitive advantages, use this fun exercise to train your team to focus on benefits:

1. Give each person a new, nicely sharpened wood pencil.

2. Tell them that you "discovered" this great new gadget at an office supply store and you think it has unlimited sales potential, but you need their help. Act as if you have never seen this neat creation before and have some fun.

3. Make a chart with two columns. At the top left, write "Features." On the top right, write "Benefits."

4. Ask each person to study your neat, new gizmo and describe a feature. You'll hear descriptions like "long," "wooden," "cylindrical," "sharp," and so on. If they say things like, "It erases," remind them that erasing isn't a feature. Perhaps they meant, "It has a rubber tip." Write the responses on the chart.

5. After you have generated a list of features, ask them to call out some benefits of the long, wooden stick. You'll probably hear things like "You can write with it," "It's easy to hold," "It erases mistakes," and so on. Write these responses on the chart under "Benefits."

6. Then ask the group, "What would be easier to sell – a long, wooden, cylindrical thing with a rubber tip, or something that you can write with, that is easy to hold, and erases mistakes?" Obviously, you could sell the latter much more easily.

While this exercise may seem a little simplistic, it is a memorable way of teaching the value of selling benefits over features. The same rules that apply to selling pencils apply to selling design services.

Figure 6.2 *Features Versus Benefits: Wooden Stick or Writing Tool?*

"So what?"

"Well, we should have less down time and fewer change-orders."

"So what?"

"Spaces we design can be built faster at a better price."

"So what?"

"The client will save money and gain access to their completed space sooner."

That is the real benefit. Your experience on similar projects (a feature) allows your client to save money and gain access to their completed space sooner, which is a benefit (see *Figure 6.2, p. 103*).

You may think that people would be able to determine benefits for themselves, but in reality, people are too busy analyzing the situation. What seems important to you may not be important to them. You therefore have to tell them why your competitive advantage will make their lives better. Most purchases, from food and clothing to a car or BIM diagrams, are responses to the benefits people receive from the product or service offered. If you can show how your product or service can satisfy a prospect's needs, you will be far closer to the sale.

Now apply the "So what?" test to each of the competitive advantages you wrote earlier. Your competitive advantages were listed on the left side. Under "Competitive Advantages," write "Features" with a red marker. This will remind you that your competitive advantages are features, not the characteristics you should be using to sell your products or services.

At the top of the right column, write "Benefits." For each feature you listed, apply the "So what?" test. Keep asking, "So what?" until you have exhausted all your answers. At the end, you should have identified the one benefit that prospective customers can relate to. You may find that the same benefit applies to many of the competitive advantages you have listed.

As you proceed, you will find a cultural change taking place among the people involved in the brainstorming exercise. They will begin thinking in terms of benefits instead of features and finding ways to communicate the benefit of what they do for the company's clients. As they go out and promote your company, either as marketers, salespeople, or project managers, they will begin to communicate this message on a daily basis to clients, who will then be better able to relate to the services your company provides.

Figure 6.3 (p. 105) shows how the "So what?" test would reveal the benefits of the competitive advantages listed for the hypothetical interior architectural firm in *Figure 6.4 (p. 106)*.

You will probably become aware of a distinct trend emerging when you begin identifying benefits. The first is that there are relatively few benefits to which people react. The second is that you need to describe how the client receives the benefit.

The Key Selling Point

After you have identified the benefits of all of your competitive advantages, you must now identify your key selling point.

Although you may feel that many of your competitive advantages are key, it is important to identify the one that is most important because when you or your consultants are developing a website, creating advertisements, emails, direct mailers, and so on, you need to be able to prioritize your advantages. An effective marketing message must communicate one selling point clearly, and then provide additional supportive selling points if needed.

If you do nothing else when preparing marketing materials, you must be sure to communicate your key selling point. By identifying it early on, you will always know which competitive advantage must be communicated.

After you have identified the key selling point, identify a few other selling points that you feel will need to be included in your marketing communication efforts. These will probably be the three or four most important additional benefits that you identified earlier.

Always write out your selling points in sentence form. This not only allows you to write complete thoughts, it also forms the basis of your copy for your website, emails, advertisements, and other

The "So what?" Exercise

This simple question, "So What?," will forever help you be a better seller. Whether or not you ever write a word of ad copy or text on a web page, understanding how to identify the benefits of the products or services you sell will enable you to prepare better presentations, get to the sale quicker, and understand your prospects' needs faster.

Anytime you need to convert competitive advantages that are stated as features into benefits, apply the So what? test. If your competitive advantage is quality, ask, "So what?"

You may answer, "Well, when we concentrate on quality, the owner gets a better building."

Ask again, "So what?"

You will ponder the question, perhaps get a little annoyed with yourself, and then answer, "Well, a better building requires less repair and maintenance."

"So what?" you demand of yourself.

Now, starting to see the light, you answer, "Well, less maintenance means less expense for the owner."

"So what?"

"Less expense means more money."

"So what?" you ask again.

But this time, there is no answer. Congratulations! You have just arrived at the real benefit. You help your clients make more money by delivering better-quality buildings that require less repair and maintenance. Now that is a competitive advantage an owner can warm up to.

Print the words So what? in large, bold type on a sheet of paper and tape it to the wall in your office. It will always remind you to zero in on benefits whenever you sell.

Figure 6.3 *The "So what?" Exercise.*

marketing communication materials well in advance. With this kind of preparation, you will always be ready with a promotion when you need one.

Defining Your Target Audience

Once you have established your goals and objectives and identified the benefits of your competitive advantages, you need to determine your target audience, the group of people most likely to buy your products or services. Note the words, "most likely to buy." Your target audience is not every potential buyer but rather, those who would benefit most from your particular products or services, and who would respond best to your competitive advantages.

Recognizing that you probably have more than one target audience, it is a good idea to prioritize these groups in terms of primary target audience, secondary target audience, and tertiary target audience. This will help you allocate your resources, concentrating most of your time and money on reaching the primary target audience.

Demographics and Psychographics

A target audience is defined by its demographic and psychographic characteristics. Demographic characteristics are those that can be measured or quantified. They include characteristics like

Competitive Advantages	Benefits
1. We have been in business for over 30 years. In that time, we have conquered almost every design challenge.	1. Clients don't have to pay for the learning curve, and projects are completed faster and more efficiently, which saves them time and money
2. Our people have significant experience in interior architecture, for both new construction and renovation.	2. Clients don't have to pay for "rookie" mistakes, and projects are delivered faster, which helps tenants occupy their office space sooner and landlords get their rent money sooner.
3. We are innovators. We find ways to improve the construction process.	3. Whenever improvements to the process are made, clients save money and get a better quality end product.
4. We are good listeners and don't make careless mistakes.	4. More attention to detail reduces the need for change and brings the project in on time and within budget.
5. We have a flat organizational chart. Our clients work with decision-makers.	5. Decision-makers keep projects moving quickly and are less prone to making mistakes, which maximizes efficiency and expedites jobs, saving clients time and money.
6. We have a lot of people with ownership in the company.	6. When clients work directly with people have a more personal stake in the success of their projects and the reputation of their firm, they typically get better service and improved quality.
7. We are extremely service-oriented.	7. Clients receive weekly updates with a progress report updating the entire team on accomplishments, schedule compliance, and budget performance.
8. We are committed to quality.	8. A quality project requires fewer changes and repairs and less maintenance, improving the investment value of the clients' properties.
9. We are nice people to work with.	9. An experience which is typically stressful becomes much more pleasant for clients.
10. We are community-minded.	10. By helping people and businesses locally, the local economy is helped and business opportunities are created for clients. Also, by caring for others, clients feel that they are cared for as well.

Figure 6.4 *Competitive Advantages and Benefits of a Hypothetical Interior Architectural Firm.*

business type, geographic location, number of employees, annual revenue, and even specific job titles within the organization. Demographic characteristics are relatively easy to identify.

Psychographic characteristics group people into homogenous segments based on their psychological makeup and lifestyle characteristics. They might include such factors as interests, hobbies, and beliefs. Psychographic characteristics, although they are more difficult to define, are often more important than demographic characteristics. Purchasing decisions, even those made by business people, are based on how a product can satisfy the buyer's needs. Understanding prospective buyers' psychographic traits will help you understand their needs and how your product or service can satisfy those needs.

When first defining your target audience, start with broad definitions. If you are an interior architect, perhaps your primary target audience will be space users. Your secondary target audience may be building owners because they often have some influence in the selection of an interior architect. Further, you may feel commercial brokers, property managers, developers, and even interior general contractors might comprise your tertiary target market.

Once you have decided what type of people fall within your target markets, you should further narrow your definition to best suit your particular competitive advantages. Start with their demographic characteristics.

In the case of our interior architect, perhaps you are best at designing office interiors that are between 1,000 and 20,000 square feet. Furthermore, you may have determined that you want to pursue negotiated projects because you do not have the resources to prepare quantities of proposals, and you have narrowed your geographic scope to a 50-mile radius of your office to provide the best level of service.

Based on these specifics, you can narrow the demographic characteristics of your target audience. If you design office spaces between 1,000 and 20,000 square feet, you can determine the size of the companies you wish to target; you might do this by talking to a friend who is a broker and asking how many square feet of office space a typical employee occupies. The answer might be that typically, each employee uses about 200 square feet, when factoring in common areas. Doing a little math, you would then know that your target audience consists of companies having between 5 and 100 employees.

Further narrowing your target audience, you might assume that a principal or office manager in each of these companies would make decisions about hiring an interior architect. Realizing that there are more principals than office managers at the smaller firms, you might decide to target these firms. Your reason is that inquiries sent to principals will be forwarded to someone with responsibility for hiring architectural firms.

Because you have decided to pursue negotiated work, you can eliminate certain types of businesses, such as government agencies. By narrowing your geographic range to a 50-mile radius, you can identify specific counties or towns to target.

You should also narrow your secondary and tertiary target audiences in the same manner. If your secondary target audience consists of building owners, you might narrow your list of owners to those whose buildings would have space in the range you are pursuing.

You realize, however, that there is more than one decision-maker in each firm, so you should include all the principals in each firm. If, when quantifying your target audience, you determine that the total number of owners is too large to reasonably pursue, you can narrow your audience to senior principals.

In summary, for the above example, the demographic profile of your target audience might be as follows:

Primary target audience

- Office space users.

- Private sector companies with between five and 100 employees.

- People with the title of Principal.

- Companies in the nearest three counties.

Secondary target audience

- Building owners.

- All principals within those firms.

- Companies in the three nearest counties.

Tertiary target audiences

- Commercial brokerage companies.

- All brokers in those companies.

- Commercial real estate developers.

- Project management positions in those companies.

- Interior general contractors.

- Estimators in those companies.

- Project managers in those companies.

Narrowing your target audience in this way is important for at least two reasons. First, it keeps you from wasting your time chasing prospective clients who may not be a good match for your services. Second, when it comes time to develop or purchase a list of prospects, you have quantifiable parameters that a list seller can use to build a list for you.

Once you have a clear understanding of your target audience in demographic terms, you should attempt to determine their psychographic characteristics. Psychographics are not as important in business-to-business selling as they are in consumer selling; when buying consumer products, people often make purchasing decisions based on how a product satisfies some emotional need. In business, on the other hand, people buy the benefits derived from a product. Sometimes those benefits are emotional, like stress reduction, but more often than not, the benefits are business details, like saving time or money.

In this manner, it is possible to develop a loose description of the psychographic characteristics of your target audience based upon your competitive advantages. If you feel that your honest dealings with clients, and your high level of customer service are your strengths, your target audience's psychographic characteristics might include an appreciation for being taken care of by someone who is straightforward. Although you will not find such details when purchasing lists, you can learn any pertinent details about your target audience through your own research. Knowing your target audience's psychographic characteristics will help you find the best language with which to communicate to them.

Speaking to One Person

After describing your target audience's demographic and psychographic characteristics in some detail, you must try to narrow your definition to one person. This exercise, often called creating a persona, will prove tremendously valuable when you begin developing your marketing materials.

Why identify one person when even your carefully defined target audience still contains a diverse mix of people? Imagining one person helps you learn how to communicate more effectively with individuals. Which is a more effective way of communicating: speaking to a group of 1,000 people or speaking with one person? When you speak to one person, you can establish eye contact, and get to know his likes and dislikes. You can get feedback on what you are saying about your firm, and you can establish a relationship. In this way, you can customize your presentation to suit individual needs.

When you speak to a crowd, you cannot make this type of connection. You can only make general assumptions about their needs. And unless they are throwing tomatoes at you, you rarely get a sense of whether or not you are saying things that will have much impact.

If you think of your target audience in the same way, when you create your marketing materials – your website, advertisements, emails, or direct mail – you must write as if you are speaking to a single person. You are not talking to the masses but rather to one individual who will react to your message.

Try identifying your target audience as one person. Are you speaking to a man or a woman? How old is he? Is she an "influencer," someone who likes to be the first to buy things and tell friends and colleagues about their purchase experience? What is his job title? How long has she held his position? What are his hobbies? Does she play golf or tennis? How tall is he?

By doing this, you will begin to see one person in your mind, and your communication efforts will become more personal and subsequently more effective. Thus, there will be something in your message, whether written or spoken, that will appeal to every person who reads or hears it.

Developing a Creative Strategy Statement

By now, you should have established your communication objectives, determined your competitive advantages and stated them in terms of their benefits, identified your key selling point, and defined your target audience by its demographic and psychographic characteristics. In other words, you should have a fairly good sense of what you want to accomplish, what you want to say about your company, and to whom you want to speak.

Now it is time to decide how you want to say it. Before you create your marketing materials, you will need to develop a sense of the look and feel of the materials so they can best convey your competitive advantages and speak to your target audience.

The best way to do this is to develop a creative strategy statement. This statement simply explains what you want to accomplish, what you want to say, to whom you want to say it, and how you should communicate it.

The creative strategy statement does not ask you to decide what words to use, and how to design materials. It simply asks you to determine the overall look and feel of your materials. For the interior architect example mentioned earlier, a creative strategy statement may sound something like this:

Our objective is to establish preference for our services and generate sales opportunities by communicating that our company is the best interior architect for privately held companies with 5 to 100 employees, needing either new or renovated office space. We will often be speaking to people who have little experience in designing or renovating their office spaces. Because they are probably anxious about this process, we will create marketing materials that communicate how choosing us will ease their minds. We will try to use visual images and text that show how we will make their lives easier if they choose us.

You can see from this example that while specific visual images and text have not been decided, the people who create the marketing materials will have a very good sense of what you want to accomplish. In fact, ideas for visuals and copy may pop into your mind as you read it.

Writing your creative strategy statement may be a challenging task, and it may take several revisions. However, once you do it, you will have a clear idea of how you will conduct your entire marketing communication campaign.

Producing a Creative Brief

Now it is time to put all the information you have gathered into a format that can be used by your team and the consultants who are helping you develop your marketing communication materials. You should create a document called a creative brief, which is essentially an outline that lists your: (1) marketing goals and the communication objectives that will achieve them; (2) competitive advantages, stated in terms of their benefits; (3) key selling point; (4) other selling points; (5) target audience, defined in demographic and psychographic terms; and (6) creative strategy statement. *Figure 6.5 (pp. 112-113)* is an example of a creative brief.

The creative brief is a guide that takes you from where you are to where you want to be. It will give your creative team the information they need to prepare marketing communication materials that convey the right message and are delivered to the right audience.

The brief is especially helpful if more than one person or consultant is working on your marketing materials. It allows the group to work from the same strategy and create materials that will work together to accomplish the desired results. For example, if you decide to create a new logo, a website, and a publicity campaign, you may use different people to perform each of these functions. The creative brief will ensure that all of these marketing efforts will have the same look and feel and will convey the same important points.

Give a copy of your creative brief to each of the people who are developing your marketing materials, and you will see whether the elements work together. If you do not want to prepare the creative brief or any of its elements yourself, make sure that your in-house creative staff or outside consultants do it for you before they prepare any of your marketing communication materials. Have them show it to you before any action is taken. If at any time, there are questions about which direction to take, refer to the creative brief. Use it as a guide to ensure that your marketing materials are consistent and stay on track.

Ensuring Ease, Efficiency, and Effectiveness

Taking the time to determine your communication objectives, define your competitive advantages, isolate a key selling point, identify your target audience, prepare a creative strategy statement, and produce a creative platform will save you untold time and marketing dollars as you prepare your marketing communication materials. It will also ensure that everything you prepare will be as effective as it can possibly be.

Congratulations. You have graduated with honors from Marketing Communication 101. Going forward, you will be able to develop your marketing communication materials and other marketing communication efforts with confidence. ■

Creative Brief

To generate $1 million in fees within the next 24 months

Communication Objectives

- Create awareness of our company
- Create awareness of our interior architectural services
- Establish the need for our services
- Communicate the benefits of our service
- Establish a preference for our service
- Generate inquiries

Competitive advantages

1. We've conquered almost every design challenge, so clients don't have to pay for the learning curve. Our projects are completed faster and more efficiently, which saves our clients time and money.

2. Our people have significant experience in interior architecture, for both new construction and renovation, so clients don't have to pay for "rookie" mistakes. This means projects are delivered faster, which helps tenants occupy their offices faster and helps owners get their rent money sooner.

3. We find ways to improve the process, which saves time and money and provided clients a better end product.

4. We are good listeners and don't make careless mistakes. This attention to detail reduces the need for changes and brings the project in on time and within budget.

5. Our clients work with decision-makers. They keep projects moving quickly and are less prone to making mistakes, which maximizes efficiency and expedites jobs, saving clients time and money.

6. Many of our people have equity in our business. When clients work with people who have a more personal stake in the success of their projects and the reputation of their firm, clients get better service and improved quality.

7. We are very service-oriented and let clients know what is going on with their project. Clients receive weekly updates with a progress report updating the entire team on accomplishments, schedule compliance, and budget performance.

8. We deliver a quality project, which requires fewer changes and repairs and less maintenance, improving the investment value of the clients' properties.

9. We make a typically stressful experience much more pleasant for our clients.

10. We are community-minded, so by helping people and businesses locally, the local economy and our clients' businesses are helped. Clients feel that by working with a caring architect, they will be treated honestly and respectfully as well.

Key Selling Point

We've conquered almost every design challenge, so clients don't have to pay for the learning curve. Our projects are completed faster and more efficiently, which saves our clients time and money.

Other Selling Points

- We have a flat organizational chart. Our clients work with decision-makers. They keep projects moving quickly and are less prone to making mistakes, which maximizes efficiency and expedites jobs, saving clients time and money.

- We design quality projects. A quality project requires fewer changes and repairs, improving the investment value of our clients' properties.

- Our people have significant experience in interior architecture, for both new construction and renovation, so clients don't have to pay for "rookie" mistakes. This means projects are delivered faster, which helps tenants occupy their offices faster and helps owners get their rent money sooner.

Target Audience

Primary Target Audience

- Private sector companies of between 5 and 100 employees
- People with the title of Principal or Office Manager
- Companies in Sacramento, Yolo, and San Joaquin counties

Secondary target audience

- All building owners in Sacramento, Yolo, and San Joaquin counties

Tertiary target audiences

- All brokers at commercial brokerage companies in the target counties
- All project managers at commercial real estate developers in the target counties
- All estimators and project managers at interior general contractors in the target counties

Creative Strategy Statement

Our objective is to establish a preference for our services and generate sales opportunities by communicating that our company is the best interior architect for privately held companies with 5 to 100 employees, needing either new or renovated office space. We will often be speaking to people who have little experience in designing or renovating their office spaces. Because they are probably anxious about this process, we will create marketing materials that communicate how choosing us will ease their minds. We will try to use visual images and text that show how we will make their lives easier if they choose us.

Figure 6.5 *Creative Brief for a Hypothetical Interior Architectural Firm.*

Things to Think About

- When developing a marketing communication plan, remember that goals are broad and business- or marketing-related, while objectives help direct how you will use communication tactics to achieve those goals.

- Whenever you try to determine your competitive advantages or selling points, put each to the "So what?" test. Ask yourself, "So what?" for each advantage. Once you have answered, ask it again. After you have run out of answers to "So what?," you will have identified the real benefit to the buyer.

- If you create a complete and thorough marketing communication plan, it will provide all the guidance your team needs—whether it is your in-house team, an outside agency, or a group of independent consultants—to execute consistent materials that work together to accomplish your goals and objectives.

- Spend extra time defining your target audiences—there may be more than one. As an exercise, narrow it down to one individual. Picture him in your mind, and create your marketing communication materials as if you are speaking to that one person. Is it not easier to get your points across to one person when you are sitting across from them, rather than when you are speaking from a podium to a large group of people?

CHAPTER SEVEN

Implementing Your Marketing Strategy: Tactics and Tools

Things You Will Learn From This Chapter

■ How an important shift is changing the way firms communicate their messages to their audiences.

■ Tips and considerations for using a variety of marketing communication tools.

■ Techniques that A/E/C firms have used when creating successful marketing campaigns, using featured examples.

BUILDING ANY STRUCTURE REQUIRES RESEARCH to select the ideal site, consideration as to how the building will be used, and planning for the project and the design. Up to this point in the book, we have talked about the lay of the land in today's design and construction environment, the necessary market research, and the strategy and planning required to grow your firm. Now it is time for you to build.

As we outlined in previous chapters, research and planning should guide the strategies and tactics you use. Just as a construction project requires many different tools, marketing offers a variety of tactics to build business. This chapter explores the tools firms can use to communicate their expertise, attract clients, and nurture relationships. It is divided up into two main sections and addresses two broad areas:

- *Building brand reputation and relationships with audiences:* Tools firms can use to build awareness. When we think of target audiences, we often think of clients, both potential and existing. However, keep in mind that a firm's audience can also include teaming partners, potential employees, and members of the media.

- *Responding to the RFP/RFQ process:* Tools firms use when pursuing a specific project opportunity, often responding to a request for proposals (RFP) or a request for qualifications (RFQ).

Today's marketing tools allow firms to easily share content across multiple platforms, and to link tactics with one another. While this has always been the case in some ways (for example, mailing a reprint of an article you were quoted in), online tools have opened new doors. With that in mind, this chapter concludes with an "Ideas for Integration" section with suggestions for tying tools together.

When implementing these tactics, carefully weigh the use of outside experts versus in-house talent to get the right blend of creativity and value. Qualified consultants and professionals can create powerful and effective content and materials through planning, strategy, and implementation.

Whether you choose to work with an outside consultant or produce your materials and content internally, consider the following dynamics and guidelines.

Building Brand Reputation and Relationships with Audiences

A Shift in Marketing Messages

Much has changed since the first edition of *A/E/C Marketing Fundamentals* was published. While advertising, direct mail, and brochures are still used by many A/E/C firms, advances in technology have opened up new ways to communicate with audiences. With customer relationship management systems (CRMs) and the ability to produce and view content on phones, tablets, and social media platforms, we all have the ability to self-publish.

As everyone is regularly inundated with messages and information, marketers must communicate relevance and customize their approaches. Rather than pushing out sales messages — "outbound marketing"— companies are focusing on inbound marketing, a system of creating engaging and helpful content that generates and nurture leads by bringing prospects in.

Examples of traditional outbound marketing include advertising, sending brochures, and cold calling; the communication is typically one-way as the company pushes out a sales message. While outbound marketing tactics are still being used today, customers are seeking more control and an inbound marketing approach using blogs, white papers, ebooks, and social media, is gaining a foothold.

Several of the tools discussed in this chapter represent an integral part of inbound marketing–content marketing. According to the Content Marketing Institute, "Content marketing is a marketing technique of creating and distributing relevant and valuable content to attract, acquire, and engage a clearly defined and understood target audience–with the objective of driving profitable customer action." In other words, it is creating and sharing content to attract clients and reinforce your identity and your brand.

You should be able to come up with topics that will help your clients and prospects consider and/ or select your firm's services. These efforts will reinforce the networking and trust-building strategies discussed in Chapter 4. Some firms are afraid to do this because they think they are "giving away their work," but keep in mind that a small amount of goodwill goes a long way. People will read your helpful articles; they'll see your name often, keeping you at the top of their mind. Additionally, your subject matter will help position you as an expert on that topic. If you feel that by showing clients what you do, they will be tempted to do it themselves, rest assured that this is unlikely. Your firm consists of experts who will save them time, and do the job well.

Content can take many forms, some of which A/E/C firms have been using for years, like conference presentations and media relations, and some that have advanced with technology and the ability to self-publish in an online setting. Previous chapters talked about the importance of research and planning. Before discussing these specific tools, here are some additional considerations.

The Importance of Brand

Communicating a distinct message has become more important than ever as clients feel the financial pressure to select firms with the lowest fees. Articulating your firm's brand and the value you bring to clients helps potential clients differentiate between companies. The more you emphasize these differences, the more likely your firm will be taken seriously.

A firm's brand is much more than its logo, colors, and choice of font. A firm's brand is its reputation—what people think of when they think about your firm, based on their experiences.

Building a brand requires consistency. When thinking about your content, make sure it passes the brand test, so that you are building your brand rather than detracting from it. Create a brand manual that outlines how to use (and how not to use) the company logo and associated elements of your corporate identity, and educate employees on its use. Regardless of the marketing tool, place a high priority on good writing, quality photography, and solid design principles.

As mentioned previously, conducting a perception survey can give you an idea of what clients and prospects think of your firm, and what makes it unique. You can conduct an internal perception survey as well to see what members of your firm think, and have strategic discussions about the firm's aspirations. The gaps that may exist in between people's perceptions and the company's aspirations can be opportunities in disguise, allowing you to set new goals to narrow those gaps through various marketing strategies and tactics.

Your Audience

When determining the content you will create or the messages you want to send in your marketing materials, you should first consider the audience. Who makes up your audience? What issues are they most interested in? What would make their jobs easier? What would be helpful for them to know? What is relevant to them? What questions do they often have? What type of content would be appealing to them? Start with your audience and make sure you're keeping their needs in mind throughout the process of creating marketing content. Focus on what is in it for them.

When thinking through each tool, also think about your desired result. For example, what do you want prospects or clients to do as a result of reading your white paper? What is the call to action you can integrate into each piece of marketing material or content?

Your Stories

To create content marketing, you need content! Rather than focusing on sharing what projects your firm has completed and what components were included in those projects, look through the lens of your audience and think about the stories those projects created. What was the specific challenge, and how did you work with the client to overcome it? What creative ideas did you bring to the table that could be applied

> **TIPS & POINTERS**
>
> When working on content with technical staff who are often busy serving clients on projects, it can often be helpful if a writer interviews them and writes a draft, rather than asking the technical professional to take the first pass at writing.

to future projects? What lessons learned from this project would benefit others? Pull the experiences from your experience, illustrating how it will benefit your audience.

The Tools

Now that you have thought through the brand you want to communicate, what will interest your audience, and what stories you have to tell, it is time to find specific places for those stories. Because a variety of marketing tools exist, you can apply the same topic in many different ways, by reaching different audiences, providing brand consistency, and making the process of content creation and dissemination more efficient and productive. This does not mean you should duplicate content word-for-word; rather, you should look at how technology and strategic thinking can help you get more use out of your stories and content by adjusting and customizing it according to the setting. Here are some of the specific tactics and tools you can use, along with tips on how to use them effectively.

Advertising

Advertising can take many shapes, appearing in directories, publications, social media, mobile applications, signage, and broadcast media. Although broadcast advertising is common in consumer marketing and some business-to-business marketing, it is not heavily used in the A/E/C realm. In general, advertisements in trade publications and directory ads for professional organizations are more commonly used. When appropriate, this can be another tool to build awareness that reaches a broad group of people within a target audience.

When producing advertisements, you can control the message but it generally has limited credibility. Frequency is important in establishing name recognition and reputation, and advertising often comes at a high cost. Another challenge is that with all of the content produced today, advertising can get lost in the shuffle. Many trade publications have special "advertorial" sections that consist of project profiles or columns; quality and helpfulness to the reader is important when creating content for this purpose.

Here are some tips when selecting the right medium in which to advertise:

- Once you have defined your target audience, think about the media they consume that might influence them.

- Make your selection based on which outlet has the readers, listeners, users, or viewers that best match your target audience and have the most credibility.

- For display ads, make sure the copy and visuals work in concert to convey your message and grab attention.

- Consider ever-evolving online forms of advertising, such as Google AdWords, social media advertisements, and promoted posts, based on your audience and marketing goals.

Example 1 (p. 137): MKK Consulting Engineers, Inc. advertises regularly in *Colorado Real Estate Journal,* which features different markets for each edition. They choose the editions that align with their markets and customize their ads accordingly. According to Kim Robertson of MKK, the firm sees an increase in Denver-area visitors to their website during the week the publication comes out, so in addition to customizing their ad for the market focus, they also update their social media accounts and website home page with images and content related to that market.

Blogs

Your blog offers an opportunity to share short articles with your audiences and to engage with them by taking comments. Like other tactics described in this chapter, the most effective blogs do not just blast out company news and announcements; they help audiences and offer differing points of view.

- Make blogs brief and on-point. If blog posts get too long, consider breaking them up (this will also help fill out your content calendar. (*See Figure 7.1* below).

The Content Calendar

One tool firms can use to make the process of managing content a little easier is a content calendar. A content calendar is a framework for you to outline all the types of content you will produce over a period of time. A content calendar can include:

- Goals of the content you'll share;

- Topics for the content;

- Properties of each type of content (Who are you targeting? What brand attributes of your firm are you focusing on?);

- Authors of the content;

- Distribution (Where the content will be distributed? A blog? An article pitch? An industry conference?); and

- Dates: Deadlines and publication dates.

Once you lay out all the content and break it down into regular intervals, it feels, and is, a lot more manageable. Including all the content you'll produce in one calendar helps you keep an eye on both internal and external deadlines (like calls for presentations and your internal blog, for example). It helps you see opportunities for integration and re-use of topics.

Figure 7.1 *The Content Calendar.*

- Link to other online sources when applicable.

- Use social media or email to drive traffic to your blog.

- With the opportunity for engagement through comments comes a responsibility to respond. Understand that not all comments on your blog post will be positive, and address comments promptly.

Example 2 (p. 138): According to Marty Wessler, PE, CEO of Wessler Engineering, the civil and environmental engineering firm launched its blog soon after redoing its website with the help of digital agency SpinWeb. Through the use of inbound marketing software to support and measure its efforts, Wessler maintains a weekly blog that is promoted through email and social media platforms. Through questionnaires, creating personas, and brainstorming with staff, the firm blogs about topics relevant to its target audience, often including links to videos and downloadable case studies. As a sign of its success, Wessler won nine projects after the blog post titled "Uh Oh, I received a letter from IDEM [Indiana Department of Environmental Management]."

Brochures

At one point or another, just about every A/E/C firm has probably needed a brochure. Rather than producing a brochure for the sake of a brochure, it is important to outline your goals and how you want the brochure to be used. Brochures can take many forms; they can be ready to take off the shelf or email, or they can be customized packages that use a variety of interchangeable, individual pages (which provides flexibility and up-to-date information but takes more time). *See Figure 7.2* below.

Figure 7.2: *EDI Landscape, LLC of Hartford, CT received first place in the 2014 SMPS Marketing Communications Awards Program in the brochure category.*

- Keep it simple; avoid the temptation to say everything about your firm in the brochure.

- Use large, dramatic photographs and short, punchy text.

- Proof your brochure several times and have more than one person review it. If you're having brochures printed, go to the printer to inspect press sheets.

- Resist the urge to take the brochure to a meeting with a client and walk them through it. While a brochure can be sent ahead of time or left behind after a meeting, if you can customize materials to send as a follow-up based on the meeting, it provides another touch point and allows you to communicate relevant content.

Direct Mail Campaigns

While hard copy, mailed materials have declined over the years, many firms continue to use hard copy mailers because they give recipients something tangible. Like email campaigns, direct mail can be used to help meet a variety of communication goals.

- The outside packaging is extremely important, as it is a first impression that will determine whether or not the recipient opens it.

- The direct mail campaign should be relevant, engaging, and something of perceived value.

- Formats can drive postage costs; be sure to coordinate carefully.

Example 3 (pp. 138-139): When trying to attract one of their priority clients, England-Thims and Miller (ETM) used a direct mail campaign to increase name recognition and position the firm as an expert in transportation planning, design, and construction engineering services. After researching marketing campaigns, ETM's team determined that a postcard with something attached would be retained 60 percent more than a stand-alone postcard. They came up with a theme comparing transportation signage with issues and solutions for successful project delivery and conducted a 10-part postcard campaign, designed in-house by ETM's art director Scott Merrell; each card contained a magnet in the shape of the featured signage and the ETM web address. To receive the last two magnets, recipients had to go online and request them. Technical business developers hand-delivered the final two magnets, allowing for an additional client contact. According to Jennifer Yoder, former business director of ETM (currently vice president at JRB Engineering), 40 percent of the target audience visited the web page to request the additional magnets. Web hits doubled in the three days following the receipt of each postcard, and ETM received direct client calls from more than 10 top priority clients to talk about a specific postcard. ETM also won several projects dealing directly with the cards' content. Three years after the campaign was introduced, ETM's staff continues to receive requests for magnet sets from their clients and often finds them displayed in clients' offices. Through this campaign, ETM demonstrated use of best practices and creativity while incorporating a method to track effectiveness by tying it into an online destination.

Email Campaigns

Firms use email on a regular basis to communicate, and many firms also use email programs to send out graphically formatted newsletters, firm announcements, messages to increase awareness of the firm, and links to additional content. Email eliminates paper and postage and allows you to track how many recipients opened your message, forwarded it, or clicked on links within it. There are many easy-to-use programs that provide templates, list storage, and analytics to quantify this data for you.

> ## TIPS & POINTERS
>
> Quality photography is key in our visually oriented society. Choose photographers that specialize in your subject matter. Talk with team members during the early stages of a project to see if collaborating on a photo shoot is a possibility.

- Make sure you have permission to send email to your list and that you're in compliance with all privacy laws.

- Take the opportunity to segment your lists so that your audiences will receive the most relevant information. For example, if you work for the higher education, K-12 school, and healthcare markets and wrote an article on the latest developments in outpatient healthcare facilities, you may only want to email a link to that article to your healthcare list.

- A short, catchy, specific, and relevant subject line improves open rates. For example, "10 trends impacting the design of healthcare facilities" says a lot more than "The latest article from Firm XYZ."

- Customize emails with the recipients' names if possible. This calls for care in terms of the integrity of the data in your list.

- Pay attention to the open rate (the number of recipients who opened or viewed your email) and the click-through rate (the percentage of recipients who clicked at least one link in your email). Evaluate your campaigns to see if there are any trends.

Exhibits

Firms use exhibits to promote themselves at trade shows and conferences. Exhibits provide an opportunity to build awareness and a database of contacts. However, making the expense worth your while requires good planning and follow-up.

- Define your objectives and know what target audience you expect to reach at the show.

- Plan pre-show communication to generate interest.

- Be creative with giveaways that will be used and retained.

- Design an interesting exhibit that will generate traffic.

- Offer something of value for prospects who provide their information.

- Staff the booth with professionals with good interpersonal and networking skills who can talk knowledgeably about your firm.

- Follow up!

Example 4 (p. 139): When Burgess & Niple (B&N), a transportation engineering, architecture, and planning firm, planned its participation in Ohio Transportation Engineering Conference (OTEC), an Ohio transportation conference, they set three goals: (1) building stronger client relationships by promoting thought leadership and fostering client-to-staff interaction in the exhibit booth; (2) increasing brand awareness for B&N's complete transportation system solutions and longevity with its 100 year anniversary; and (2) securing two new contracts. While previous booths focused on current projects and the firm, the approach at OTEC focused on problems that the firm's clients were facing (aging infrastructure and the health of the Ohio economy) and B&N's approach to help them solve those problems through innovative solutions. The creative team crafted the booth message, "From Diagnosis to CURE. Complete Transportation Solutions for a Healthier Ohio." Additional tactics included sending a pre-conference email to 250 clients and teaming partners, using survey software at the booth, presenting at three sessions, using Twitter and a custom hashtag for their gift card drawing, and following up with attendees. According to B&N's Rachel Headings, CPSM, the firm collected over 20 qualified leads and 30 contacts from the survey, signed three new clients (one with no request for proposal issued), engaged with over 150 clients in the booth, client event, and sessions, and reinforced their brand awareness, receiving direct feedback from clients and consultants on the "fresh approach" of the booth and their use of Twitter.

Newsletters and Self-published Magazines

Content can be delivered in many ways, including being decentralized through social media updates, email announcements, or blogs or compiled in regular publications, either online or in print. Newsletters and magazines provide the opportunity to tell important, educational, enlightening, or entertaining stories that connect firms with their audiences on a regular basis. The goal is to create something clients look forward to reading, rather than hitting the delete key or tossing it into the trash. Newsletters are traditionally thought of as sharing company news, whereas magazines generally focus on helpful articles about industry trends and feature rich graphics and photos. In both cases, relevant content and good design are essential. *(See Figure 7.3, p. 128)*

- When producing anything on a schedule, planning is essential so that you are not scrambling to fill pages with content, but instead are delivering information of value.

- Consider headlines, subheadings, call-out boxes, and captions carefully – people usually read them before the body text.

- The design needs to capture attention and help the reader focus on the articles.

Example 5 (p. 140): Barton Malow Company produces an external client newsletter that they distribute electronically through an email announcement. Recipients can click into the stories they are interested in. In addition, the company does a small print run for select contacts and for special occasions. For example, when Barton Malow features LEAPS (their internship program), in their newsletter, they print brochures to handout at career fairs as well. In total, this issue alone was viewed electronically more than 3,000 times. The Barton Malow marketing team produces the newsletter in-house, with multiple staff members contributing to the writing, photography, email creation, etc. Dana Galvin Lancour, FSMPS, CPSM of Barton Malow, said the team is proud of their email open rate of approximately 36 percent and their click-through rate of 26 percent.

Figure 7.3: *Syska Hennessy Group, Inc. of Fairfax, VA received first place in the 2014 SMPS Marketing Communications Awards Program in the Magazine category.*

Presentations

Presentations are effective tools to showcase thought leadership to potential and existing clients and partners. They can be delivered in person at industry events, in an office, or through web-based platforms. In addition, presentations help advance the industry through showcasing best practices and new ways of thinking.

- When developing presentations, consider asking a client to co-present with your firm representative to add another perspective and further the relationship.

- Learn who will be in the audience and what level of background they might have regarding your subject.

- Pre-designed bulleted templates have a tendency to drive how presentations look. Rather than starting with a template, focus on your message first and then use graphics and presentation tools to support the message. The image becomes a backdrop that supports your message, rather than the visual controlling what you say and becoming the focus.

- When you're the speaker, build in plenty of preparation and practice time so you're comfortable with the content. Consider engaging the help of a presentation coach to refine your skills.

- In addition to in-person presentations, consider webinars, videos, and podcasts that allow participants to receive the information at their convenience.

Public and Media Relations

Publicity and earned media (being quoted in the news media or invited to write an article for a trade publication), positions your firm as an expert while providing credibility and third party validation. If you can get an article placed in a publication, you pay only whatever it costs you to prepare it. Keep in mind, however, that there is no guarantee that the media will use your story. In addition, you cannot control the message like you can in advertising, self-published content, or direct mail. You may send a carefully worded press release to the media, and the publication may use only a small amount of the information. Or you may provide quotes to a reporter and find them used in a story in a way that does not convey your true intention. If you are planning to use publicity as part of your marketing mix, you must be prepared for this risk and understand how to deal with it.

- Focus your efforts by targeting magazines or newspapers that focus on issues of importance to your target audience.

- Know the publication, what kinds of articles they accept, and how they like to be contacted.

- Review the publication's editorial calendar to see what topics they are covering and how your subject matter could fit in.

- If the publication accepts authored articles, write a short pitch first to propose your idea. If the editor is interested, she will follow up with more direction.

- Conduct media training for company spokespeople and the experts you're pitching.

- Once your article has been placed, link it to other tactics to notify your contacts about the article.

Self-Sponsored Seminars

Developing and hosting an in-house seminar on topics relevant to your clients' markets can be a powerful inbound marketing tool. It allows clients to visit your office, receive content that will benefit their organizations, and network with like-minded attendees. Provide professional development hours and include guest presenters outside of your organization to increase the credibility of the event.

- Consider charging a nominal admission. People value what they pay for, it will make the event more exclusive, and it will help you keep track of RSVPs.

- Consider an issue-oriented keynote address to set the stage for later parts of the seminar.

- Weigh the advantages of presenting your own firm's thought leadership as seminar content versus providing speakers from outside the firm. Each approach has its own appeal and credibility.

- Determine if sponsors will be necessary to defray costs. If so, plan what benefits they will receive from sponsorship and make sure they take advantage of them.

- Consider recording the event for future distribution or streaming it for a different pricing structure to those who may not be attend in person.

Social Media

Social media platforms such as LinkedIn, Twitter, and Facebook can be effective at driving people to other online destinations, such as blogs, articles, and videos. A variety of social media platforms exist to help companies share content and connect with the audience, and different members of your audience will use different tools. Rather than diving into any social media platform because it is the latest and greatest, firms should do their due diligence to determine which platform is appropriate to their audience and how to integrate tools to share content in multiple ways.

- Determine which platforms are the best to use based on your audience and your goals; do not just jump on the newest ones.

- Personal brand is important in professional services marketing. Professional social media profiles provide an online presence for your staff and another opportunity to showcase their personal brands and expertise.

- Share best practices with your company to help them use social media intelligently and effectively.

- Take time to organize and use dashboards and programs that allow you to create lists of connections whose updates you do not want to miss.

- Be open to serendipity, but stay focused on your plan and strategy.

- It can be helpful to structure some social media time into your day so you use your time wisely. Consider batching tasks, limiting time on social media to stay focused, turning off notifications if they distract you while still checking in at regular intervals, and setting up alerts to find out when people mention you or your firm.

- Consider not only creating content but sharing content prepared by others. When you read articles that you feel would be helpful to your audience, share them.

- Social media is an excellent listening tool. In addition to sharing content, read content shared by your audience members. Converse with your connections so you stay at the top of their mind and make them feel appreciated and listened to.

Videos

Videos can be effective when your firm has a story to tell visually. In addition, video can easily be promoted online through social media shares and when done well, has the potential to go viral.

- Once you have come up with a concept for your video, storyboarding can help you organize your thoughts.

- The focus should be on producing content that is engaging, interesting, and helpful to your audience—not a sales pitch.

- Given people's short attention span, brevity is key. There is a plethora of information available to us, and the quest for relevant content competes for people's attention.

- When shooting your video, keep in mind that many will be viewing it on mobile devices with smaller screens.

Example 6 (p. 141): SmithGroupJJR used YouTube videos to achieve several goals. According to Kate Erdy, CPSM, formerly of SmithGroupJJR, in addition to announcing its Washington, DC office relocation, the videos were designed to communicate the firm's understanding of workplace design and change management, as well as to showcase workplace practice leaders in the DC office. The audience consisted of all of the firm's DC clients and national workplace clients. Promoted through email, social media, and on the firm's new website home page, the (re)locate campaign consisted of a documentary-style video series of five episodes: (re)asons, (re)design, (re)use, (re)move, and (re)act, all designed and produced in-house.

Websites

Having a web presence is essential in today's business environment, since many potential clients qualify your firm by visiting your website. It is important to make your website an engaging, easy-to-navigate, content-rich, and frequently updated source of information that speaks to your firm's brand.

- Keep up-to-date on the often-changing methods of search engine optimization (SEO) practices to make your website appear high on the list of results returned by a search engine; this helps maximize the number of visitors to your website.

- Tie your website to social media and other communication outlets you use.

- Update your website often.

- Keep content concise and on-point.

- Place a high priority on quality photography and graphics.

- Make sure contact information is clear.

- Design your website to be responsive so it adapts to various devices.

- Use analytics to determine where website visitors are spending the most time and evaluate improvements based on that information.

Example 7 (p. 141): When Primera redesigned its website, it focused on conveying the message of a unified, full-service regional firm focused on providing exceptional expertise and service in three areas: buildings, transportation, and power. With the help of branding firm Miles Design, Primera followed several trends for its distinct, content-focused website, including responsive design, simplified icons, and flat design elements along with a clean aesthetic and bold new colors. An email announcement communicated the new website, the new URL (http://www.primeraeng.com), new email addresses, and the firm's opening of two new offices. With a target audience of clients and candidates, Primera's goals included engaging users and supporting recruitment efforts. According to Primera's Matt Dvorak, the new website's career section increased the number of résumé submissions from five to nearly 200 per month. The number of users spending five minutes or more on the website increased more than 25 percent over the previous website.

White Papers and Reports

White papers can be excellent tools for exploring more in-depth topics and have increased perceived value. It is appropriate to write a white paper or report when you have a complex topic you can explore from different angles. Consider adding a research component to add value to the content.

- Take advantage of capturing data by allowing visitors to your website to download the white paper or report.

- Quality of writing and organization is key. Use bullet points, headlines, and subheads.

- Consider partnering with clients to help them tell their stories.

Determining Effectiveness

As marketers, we need to invest in activities that help us advance toward our goals. While it is challenging to determine hard numbers on marketing tools' return on investment because of the multiple touch points it takes to eventually result in a project engagement, there are ways to monitor progress. Online tools also allow you to track open rates, website traffic, and engagement levels. Perception surveys conducted before and after targeted campaigns can help marketers determine if opinions about firms have changed. It is also important to connect the dots that eventually lead to opportunities. Maintaining a dialogue with clients about where they heard about you and capturing that anecdotal data can help determine if your efforts are being noticed.

TIPS & POINTERS

The reader typically looks at headlines, photo captions, and call-out boxes first. Use these items, as well as bullets, strategically to convey key messages.

Responding to the RFP/RFQ Process

Once a potential client or project has been identified, many tools come into play to support the pursuit of that project. Customization, thought leadership, and brand continue to play a large role in this part of the process.

The Importance of Intelligence and Customization

As we have emphasized in earlier chapters, you must gather intelligence about your clients and their potential projects, and it is critical to do this long before a request for qualifications or request for proposals has come out. The capture plan is another tool firms can use to gather information about potential clients and projects. (see *Figure 7.4, p. 134*). If you wait until the RFQ or RFP has been issued, it is often too late to get the information you need, get to know the decision-makers, and position your firm effectively. It is also important to have a solid go/no go process so that you can determine if a project opportunity is worth pursuing. If you do decide to "go," make sure the intelligence you have been gathering is then applied and addressed in your marketing materials.

In the SMPS Foundation book, *A/E/C Business Development: The Decade Ahead,* which features findings from sellers and buyers of professional services, one of the buyers interviewed said that she wants to know that firms have done their homework. She wants you to know her community and her organization and what makes it unique, and she can spot boilerplate a mile away. As marketers, we must work to gain a thorough understanding of our client and then illustrate that understanding through our materials.

In addition to being customized, make sure your responses are compliant and concise. Clients are receiving and reviewing a multitude of responses – make yours stand out by being easy to navigate and relevant.

- Organize your response based on the structure of the request.

- Follow the instructions and make sure you have responded to everything the client has asked for.

- A bigger proposal does not make a better proposal. Include only the information most relevant to the client.

Proposals and Statements of Qualifications

When a request for a proposal or request for qualifications is issued, it is time to translate the information you have learned into a customized response that resonates with the client. Some of the typical items requested in an RFQ include:

- Executive summary.

- Firm overview.

- Project approach.

- Organizational chart of team.

- Résumés of team members.

- Similar project examples.

- Proposed fee (usually called a request for proposal).

- Additional information such as certificates of insurance, proof of registration, and litigation history.

The capture plan is another tool firms can use to gather information about potential clients and projects.

The capture plan should be updated regularly and used during strategy meetings to identify information to be gathered and to make assignments.

Some of the items a capture plan can include:

- Client contacts, their top issues or concerns, and who has a relationship with the contacts.

- Additional influences outside of the client organization.

- Top issues for the client organization.

- Members of the firm's strategy team.

- Potential team members and their strengths and weaknesses.

- Benefits the firm brings to address the clients' issues and priorities.

- Competitors and the benefits they bring.

- Tasks, assignments, and due dates.

Figure 7.4 *The Capture Plan.*

All of these items should be consistent in style and tone to help you communicate your brand.

Cover Letter

A cover letter is an effective way to set the stage for the proposal or statement of qualifications. Resist the urge to start out the cover letter with "We are pleased to present" or some other generic opening. Take the opportunity to show distinction with a unique opening that recognizes your client's priorities and previews how your team can address them.

A cover letter can serve as an executive summary, or you can choose to have a brief cover letter and then go more in-depth on your executive summary. The choice depends on the preferences of the client (if they specify an executive summary) and the amount of information you need to address.

Project Descriptions

Firms' project sheets typically consist of the project name and location, photographs, a narrative describing the project, and a bulleted list of statistics like construction cost, completion date, and size. Rather than focusing solely on components of the project, differentiate your firm by seeking out the stories of each project. What were the specific challenges the owner faced, and how did the team address them? Show examples, through stories and statistics, of how your firm provided value, and communicate those in the narrative. In addition, take the opportunity to customize project sheets and showcase why they are included as relevant experience. For example, use a call-out box to draw attention to common attributes between the project you're pursuing and the project you're featuring.

Team

It is important to demonstrate that teams and individuals have worked together successfully on projects in the past. When gathering project information, take the time to learn and document which other firms worked on the project so you can take note of that when teaming with those firms on future pursuits.

Résumés

Firms' résumés typically consist of a short narrative, a list of relevant projects, education, and registration information. As with project descriptions, when including résumés, think about why each person was selected for the team and highlight that information. If members of your team have been published or have presented on relevant topics, including these items on their résumés can add credibility and showcase their thought leadership. Customize the list of projects they have worked on to be relevant to the current pursuit. To add even more customization and relevance, include a brief statement as to why certain projects were featured.

Databases

In the throes face of a deadline, it can be tempting to go back to a similar RFQ response and repurpose it for the one at hand. This can create many challenges—old client names could be missed, the opportunity for customization might be influenced by past materials, and changes you make to update information might not go back into your master file. It is important to maintain a database with up-to-date information, including data on your firm's experience, overviews, and approaches so that you are not searching for information, and you are using the latest and greatest information. Databases that tie the time entered on time sheets to résumés allow you to quickly determine past projects that your team worked on. There are many methods to choose from, the key to success is using them diligently so that the database becomes a trusted source of information.

The Shortlist Interview

When potential clients invite you to interview for a specific project, they see the interview as a chance to evaluate your team's chemistry. According to one higher education client, he will be working with the team for three years, so the interview is an opportunity to determine who he likes and wants to work with. Sometimes the client will specify the format of the presentation; other times, firms will be given a time frame and can fill it as they wish. The same advice provided in the previous section about presentations applies here.

- Focus on the message first and then the graphics that will support it, rather than diving headfirst into the visuals.

- The team should budget plenty of time for preparation. A team that is comfortable and prepared will improve the chemistry in the room.

- Spend time thinking of questions that might be asked—especially the ones you do not want the client to ask—and determine how you will respond.

- Keep in mind that the leadership skills of the project manager will come across in the interview and make an impression with the client.

Ideas for integration

The following list provides additional ideas of how firms can integrate the various tools discussed in this chapter.

- Provide a white paper to conference or trade show attendees.

- Turn your conference presentation into a lunch-and-learn series delivered locally.

- When you have an article published in a trade publication, obtain article reprints and post them on your website or send them to prospective clients. List the article on the author's résumé and online profiles and send out a link to the article through social media updates.

- Share news about an upcoming presentation in a status update on social media outlets. Write a blog about the presentation or film a short video, capturing the top tips shared. Provide a lunch-and-learn for local clients. Share the presentation online.

- Put social media icons on your marketing materials so people know where else they can find you.

Conclusion

This chapter opened with a metaphor, comparing the process of building a structure to building a business. Both take research and planning and the use of many different tools. And, once a structure is built, it needs to be maintained and updated to respond as the needs of its users change. Follow the tips outlined in this chapter, but keep in mind that many of the tactics will evolve—some more quickly than others—due to changes in the marketplace, technology and the needs and behavior of your audiences. As marketers, it's important for us to use trusted principles that stand the test of time, yet always be looking ahead to make sure we're being responsive to our audiences—both today, and in the future. ■

Example 1: *MKK Consulting Engineers Advertisement.*

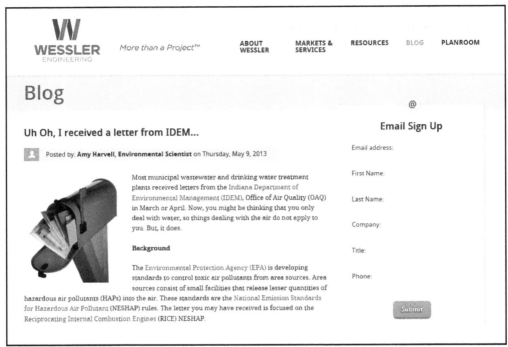

Blog

@

Uh Oh, I received a letter from IDEM...

Posted by: **Amy Harvell, Environmental Scientist** on Thursday, May 9, 2013

Most municipal wastewater and drinking water treatment plants received letters from the Indiana Department of Environmental Management (IDEM), Office of Air Quality (OAQ) in March or April. Now, you might be thinking that you only deal with water, so things dealing with the air do not apply to you. But, it does.

Background

The Environmental Protection Agency (EPA) is developing standards to control toxic air pollutants from area sources. Area sources consist of small facilities that release lesser quantities of hazardous air pollutants (HAPs) into the air. These standards are the National Emission Standards for Hazardous Air Pollutant (NESHAP) rules. The letter you may have received is focused on the Reciprocating Internal Combustion Engines (RICE) NESHAP.

Email Sign Up

Email address:

First Name:

Last Name:

Company:

Title:

Phone:

Submit

Example 2: *Wessler Engineering blog.*

Example 3: *England-Thims & Miller, Inc.(ETM) contact form and website.*

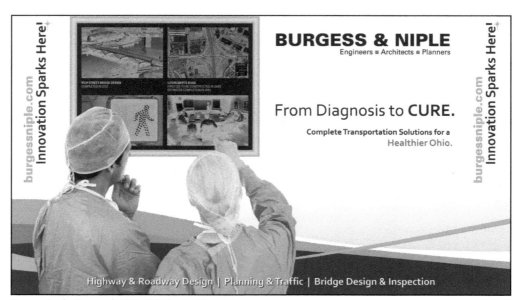

Example 4: *Burgess & Niple (B&N) advertisement.*

In this year's back to school issue of Marvels, you will find a focused view of our LEAPS (LEArning Practicum for Students) internship program. Follow the experiences of our interns, what they learn, the projects they engage in and the people they work with during this 12-week intensive and hands-on program. Our featured interns, as well as our Class of 2013, join us from universities across the country and are sent to projects throughout our markets and geography.

To find out more about our overall program, please check out last year's issue, which laid the foundation for us to focus on the people beginning their careers with Barton Malow.

In this Issue....

Published by LEAPS
LEArning Practicum for Students

LEAPS Class of 2013

Life in the Field
Rob Henry, Purdue University

Embracing Change
Abby Kreider, Penn State University

Partnership in Action
Mike Stanbary, Purdue University & Stephen Ungerleider, University of Virginia

Technology Accelerator
Jose Sandoval, Purdue University & Nicco Buffone, Michigan State University

Energy for the Future
Aurelia Yazzie, Purdue University

Innovators - Technology Applied
Sheila McLaughlin, Florida State University

2012 LEAPS Issue
Read last year's edition of the LEAPS issue of Marvels

f Follow our LEAPS Facebok Page

Example 5: *Barton Malow's LEAPS email marketing newsletter.*

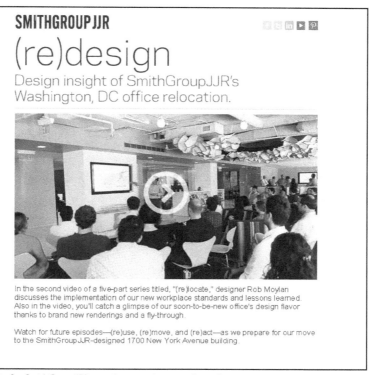

Example 6: *SmithGroupJJR's email announcing one of its videos.*

Example 7: *Primera Engineers, Ltd's website as of 2015. (Photo on website by Matty Wolin)*

Things to Think About

- What is your audience interested in? What information would be helpful for them to know so that they could do their jobs better? Does it pass the "what is in it for them" test?

- What content are you producing at your firm that you could repurpose and tie into additional communication outlets? How can you integrate and link tools together for increased effectiveness?

- Do your marketing materials communicate distinction? Do they reflect your brand? Do they communicate the value you can provide to clients?

GLOSSARY

2D (two-dimensional) are drawings on paper (X, Y plane) that present buildings in a variety of views showing height and width, height and depth, or width and depth such as floor plans, elevations, sections, ceilings and detail drawings.

3D (three dimensional) are drawings (X, Y, Z plane) that present buildings in a variety of views showing height, width and depth.

Augmented reality (AR) is a live direct or indirect view of a physical, real-world environment whose elements are augmented (or supplemented) by computer-generated sensory input such as sound, video, graphics or GPS data. With the help of advanced AR technology (e.g. adding computer vision and object recognition), the information about the surrounding real world of the user becomes interactive and digitally manipulable. Artificial information about the environment and its objects can be overlaid on the real world.

Alternative project delivery (APD) provides a means to obtain upfront capital financing from the private sector, and achieve cost efficiencies throughout the full life cycle of an infrastructure asset, including design, construction, maintenance and operations.

Bid, also known as construction bidding, is the process of submitting a proposal (tender) to undertake, or manage the undertaking of a construction project. The process starts with a cost estimate from blueprints and take offs.

BIM (building information modeling) is a new way of approaching the design and documentation of building projects. The process involves the generation and management of digital representations of physical and functional characteristics of places. Current BIM software is used by individuals, businesses and government agencies who plan, design, construct, operate and maintain diverse physical infrastructures, from utilities and roads, to buildings.

The Brooks Act is a United States federal law passed in 1972 that requires that the U.S. Federal Government select engineering and architecture firms based upon their competency, qualifications and experience rather than by price.

CAD (computer-aided design) is a computer system used to assist in the creation, modification, analysis, or optimization of a design. CAD may be used to design curves and figures in two-dimensional (2D) space; or curves, surfaces, and solids in three-dimensional (3D) space. CAD helps increase the productivity of the designer, improves the quality of design, as well as streamline improve communications through documentation

Cloud computing is a recently evolved computing terminology or metaphor based on utility and consumption of computing resources. It is a type of Internet-based computing where different services – such as servers, storage and applications – are delivered to an organization's computers and devices through the Internet.

CM (Construction Manager) is hired to manage a construction project, and serves as the intermediary between his clients and his workers, between the architect and his subcontractors, and between the project and any regulatory personnel.

CMAR (Construction Management At Risk) is a project delivery method in which the Construction Manager acts as a consultant to the owner in the development and design phases, but assumes the risk for construction performance as the equivalent of a general contractor holding all trade subcontracts during the construction phase. This delivery method is also known as CM (Construction Manager) and GC (General Contractor).

The Code of Hammurabi is a well-preserved Babylonian law code of ancient Mesopotamia, dating back to about 1754 B.C. Nearly one-half of the Code deals with matters of contract, with provisions that specifically establishes the liability of a builder for a house that collapses, for example, or property that is damaged while left in the care of another. Other provisions concern household and family relationships, and military service. The code has been seen as an early example of a fundamental law regulating a government is also one of the earliest examples of the idea of presumption of innocence, and it also suggests that both the accused and accuser have the opportunity to provide evidence.

Content Marketing Institute (CMI) is an organization whose mission is to advance the practice of content marketing. http://www.contentmarketinginstitute.com

Content marketing is a marketing technique of creating and distributing valuable, relevant and consistent content to attract and acquire a clearly defined audience – with the objective of driving profitable customer action.

Contractor (also known as general contractor (GM), main contractor, construction manager (CM), prime contractor) is responsible for the day-to-day oversight of a construction website, management of subcontractors, vendors and trades, throughout the course of a building project.

CPM (Construction Project Management, also known as Construction Management) is the overall planning, coordination, and control of a project from beginning to completion. CPM is aimed at meeting a client's requirement in order to produce a functionally and financially viable project.

CPSM (Certified Professional Services Marketer) is a credential issued by SMPS. It is a voluntary certification designed to elevate one's professional standards in marketing. The CPSM designation also serves as a mark of distinction for professional services marketers and business developers, raising their standing with their employers, peers, and the public.

Creative brief is a document created through initial meetings, interviews, readings and discussions between a client and designer before any work begins. Throughout the project, the creative brief continues to inform and guide the work.

Customer relationship management system (CRM) is a system for managing a company's interactions with current and future customers. It often involves using technology to organize, automate and synchronize sales, marketing, customer service, and technical support.

DB (design-build) is when the private partner provides both design and construction of a project to the public agency. This type of partnership can reduce time, save money, provide stronger guarantees and allocate additional project risk to the private sector. It also reduces conflict by having a single entity responsible to the public owner for the design and construction. The public sector partner owns the assets and has the responsibility for the operation and maintenance.

DBB (design-bid-build) is the traditional U.S. project delivery method where an owner develops contract documents with an architect or engineer consisting of a set of blueprints and a detailed specification. Bids are solicited from contractors based on these documents; a contract is then awarded to the lowest responsive and responsible bidder.

DBM (design-build-maintain) is similar to a DB except the maintenance of the facility for some period of time becomes the responsibility of the private sector partner. The benefits are similar to the DB with maintenance risk being allocated to the private sector partner and the guarantee expanded to include maintenance. The public sector partner owns and operates the assets.

DBO (design-build-operate) is a single contract is awarded for the design, construction, and operation of a capital improvement. Title to the facility remains with the public sector unless the project is a design-build-operate-transfer or design-build-own-operate project. The DBO method of contracting is contrary to the separated and sequential approach ordinarily used in the United States by both the public and private sectors. This method involves one contract for design with an architect or engineer, followed by a different contract with a builder for project construction, followed by the owner's taking over the project and operating it.

DBOM (design-build-operate-maintain) is an integrated partnership that combines the design and construction responsibilities of design-build procurements with operations and maintenance. These project components are procured from the private section in a single contract with financing secured by the public sector. The public agency maintains ownership and retains a significant level of oversight of the operations through terms defined in the contract.

Design charrette is an intense period of design or planning activity to finish a project before a deadline.

E&O (errors and omissions) is a professional liability insurance that protects companies and individuals against claims made by clients for inadequate work or negligent actions. E&O insurance often covers both court costs, and any settlements up to the amount specified on the insurance contract.

EPC (engineering, procurement and construction) is a delivery system in which one contract is signed with an entity to provide the design required, purchasing of all of the equipment and materials and constructing the project. This approach is common in the power industry and heavy industrial markets, where there is typically some extremely costly equipment and potential alternatives to approaching the solution desired.

FSMPS (Fellow of SMPS), a designation issued by SMPS, reflects the highest level of experience and leadership in marketing within the design and building industry. The Fellows serve as a resource at the chapter, regional, and national levels, providing insight, ideas, programs, and mentoring for the benefit of the members and the Society. In addition, these individuals teach, write, and speak on marketing issues outside of SMPS, working to advance the profession of marketing professional services throughout the architectural/engineering/construction industry.

FTP (File Transfer Protocol) is a standard network protocol used to transfer computer files from one host to another host over a TCP-based network, such as the Internet.

GC (general contractor), is the contractor that signs the agreement with the owner to take responsibility for the whole project. Projects may or may not have a general contractor depending on the delivery system.

GMP (guaranteed maximum price, also known as G-Max, not-to-exceed price, NTE, or NTX) is a cost-type contract where the contractor is compensated for actual costs incurred plus a fixed fee subject to a ceiling price. The contractor is responsible for cost overruns, unless the GMP has been increased via formal change order. Savings resulting from cost underruns are returned to the owner. This is different from a fixed-price contract (also known as stipulated price contract or lump-sum contract) where cost savings are typically retained by the contractor and essentially become additional profits.

Go/no go designates the decision to continue with or abandon a course of action.

GPS (Global Positioning System) is a space-based satellite navigation system that provides location and time information in all weather conditions, anywhere on or near the Earth where there is an unobstructed line of sight to four or more GPS satellites.

HL23 is a 14 floor condominium tower located at 23rd Street in New York's West Chelsea Arts District that responds to a unique and challenging design directly adjacent to the High Line (an elevated section of a disused New York Central Railroad spur called the West Side Line), partially impacted by a spur from the elevated tracks that make up the High Line superstructure. HL23 is the first freestanding building by internationally celebrated theorist and maverick architect Neil Denari.

HMO (health maintenance organization) is an organization that provides or arranges managed care for health insurance, self-funded health care benefit plans, individuals, and other entities in the United States and acts as a liaison with health care providers (hospitals, doctors, etc.) on a prepaid basis.

HVAC (heating, ventilating, and air conditioning) is a commercial system that provides people working inside buildings with "conditioned" air so that they will have a comfortable and safe work environment.

Inbound marketing is when a company promotes its services through blogs, podcasts, video, eBooks, enewsletters, white papers, SEO, social media marketing, and other forms of content marketing which serve to attract customers.

Internal reporting system is a term used to describe the overarching framework of how internal reports are provided.

IPD (Integrated Project Delivery) is a project delivery method that contractually requires collaboration among the primary parties – owner, designer, and builder – so that the risk, responsibility and liability for project delivery are collectively managed and appropriately shared.

Key selling points can usually be classified as benefits and features, neutralizers, and counter.

Laser technology products calculate distance by measuring the time of flight of very short pulses of infrared light. This differs from the traditional surveying instrument method of measuring phase shifts by comparing the incoming wavelength with the phase of the outgoing light.

LEED (Leadership in Energy & Environmental Design) is a green building certification program under the U.S. Green Building Council (USGBC) that recognizes best-in-class building strategies and practices in the following areas: (1) sustainable websites; (2) water efficiency; (3) energy and atmosphere; (4) material and resources; (5) indoor environmental quality; and (6) innovation in design. See http://www.usgbc.org

Life cycles is a technique to assess environmental impacts associated with all the styles of a product's life from cradle to grave.

M&M (means and methods) is a term used in construction to describe the day-to-day activities a contractor employs to complete construction. M&M of construction are ordinarily understood to be covered under general liability policies, rather than professional liability policies.

Market segmentation is a marketing strategy that involves dividing a broad target market into subsets of consumers, businesses, or countries who have common needs and priorities, and then designing and implementing strategies to target them.

Marketing communications plan involves bringing all the different parts of a marketing plan together into a document that can be used as a guide during the implementation of the plan. As a key part of brand building, an integrated marketing communications plan encompasses all parts of a marketing campaign, from the product's background and description of the target market to print advertising and online promotions, and should offer a well-researched and effective method to get your message about your product or service to your target market at the most effective time and place.

Marketing communications tells your story and supports your business all while ensuring the right messages are sent to the right audience and accurately reflect your brand.

Marketing mix is a combination of factors that can be controlled by a company to influence consumers to purchase its products.

Mission statement defines what an organization is, why it exists, its reason for being. At a minimum, a mission statement should define who your primary customers are, identify the products and services you produce, and describe the geographical location in which you operate.

Model-driven prefabrication describes the use of the BIM model to enable prefabrication and assembly of building components both off and on the construction website.

Modularization is a process that determines the simplest meaningful parts that compose a task. There is no formal process to implement modularization, and in practice, it is very arbitrary.

NCPPP (The National Council for Public-Private Partnerships) is a non-profit, non-partisan organization founded in 1985 whose mission is to advocate and facilitate the formation of public-private partnerships at the federal, state and local levels, and to raise the awareness of governments and businesses of the means by which their cooperation can cost effectively provide the public with quality goods, services and facilities. www.ncppp.org

Networking is when people interact with each other to exchange information and develop contacts, especially to further one's career.

Outbound marketing is a traditional form of marketing where a company initiates the conversation and sends its message out to an audience. Outbound marketing examples include: tradeshows, TV commercials, radio commercials, print advertisements (newspaper ads, magazine ads, flyers, brochures, catalogs, etc.), cold calls, and email blasts.

PPP (public–private partnership, also known as P3) is a project delivery system in which a private entity or developer takes a part in financing a construction project in return for monetary compensation.

Primary research consists of a collection of original primary data collected by the researcher. It is often undertaken after the researcher has gained some insight into the issue by reviewing secondary research or by analyzing previously collected primary data such as questionnaires, surveys, telephone interviews, observations, and ethnographic research.

Primary target audience is the segment of a marketplace a business believes will give it the best chance to sell. A primary target market may not be the largest segment of a marketplace.

Productize is to take a new service, product or product feature that a company has provided to a single customer or a few customers on a custom basis, and turn it into a standard, fully tested, packaged, supported and marketed product.

Project delivery method is a system used by an agency or owner for organizing and financing design, construction, operations, and maintenance services for a structure or facility by entering into legal agreements with one or more entities or parties. Examples include DB, DBB, DBOM and IPD.

Psychographics is the study of personality, values, opinions, attitudes, interests, and lifestyles. Because this area of research focuses on interests, attitudes, and opinions, psychographic factors are also called IAO variables.

RFI (request for information) is a standard business process whose purpose is to collect written information about the capabilities of various suppliers. Normally it follows a format that can be used for comparative purposes.

RFID (radio frequency identification) is a technology that incorporates the use of electromagnetic or electrostatic coupling in the radio frequency (RF) portion of the electromagnetic spectrum to uniquely identify an object, animal, or person.

RFP (request for proposal) is a solicitation made often through a bidding process, by an agency or company interested in procurement of a commodity, service or valuable asset, to potential suppliers to submit business proposals. It is submitted early in the procurement cycle, either at the preliminary study, or procurement stage.

RFQ/P (Request for Qualifications/Proposals) refers to the pre-qualification stage of the procurement process. Only those proponents who successfully respond to the RFQ and meet the qualification criteria will be included in the subsequent Request for Proposals (RFP) solicitation process. Some firms find this two-staged approach helps to both streamline the solicitation process, and to gather information about candidates for future use. In most cases, when the requirements for a project are uncomplicated, an RFQ is all that is required to determine the appropriate candidate.

Risk matrix is probably one of the most widespread tools for risk evaluation. They are mainly used to determine the size of a risk and whether or not the risk is sufficiently controlled.

Secondary research involves the summary, collation and/or synthesis of existing research from third-party sources such as marketing research reports, company websites, magazine articles, and other sources. By far the most widely used method for collecting data, this process involves collecting data from either the originator or a distributor of primary research. In other words, it means accessing information

Secondary target audience is that portion of a business' total potential customers second most likely to purchase its product. They differ from the most populous and profitable, primary target audience in characteristics, behavior and number. Though it does not generate as much revenue, the secondary target audience is worth marketing efforts because of its relation to, and potential influence on, the primary target audience.

SEO (search engine optimization) is the process of affecting the visibility of a website in a search engine's "natural" or un-paid ("organic") search results. In general, the earlier (or higher ranked on the search results page), and more frequently a website appears in the search results list, the more visitors it will receive from the search engine's users.

Simulation is the imitation of the operation of a real-world process or system over time. The act of simulating something first requires that a model be developed; with the model representing the key characteristics or behaviors/functions of the selected physical or abstract system or process.

Situation analysis refers to a collection of methods that managers use to analyze an organization's internal and external environment to understand the organization's capabilities, customers, and business environment.

Social media is defined as a group of Internet-based applications that build on the ideological and technological foundations of Web 2.0 that allows the creation and exchange of user-generated content. As of 2014, the largest social networks in the Internet are Facebook, Twitter, Instagram, LinkedIn, and Pinterest.

Social media marketing is the process of gaining website traffic or attention through social media websites.

Spearin Doctrine is a legal principle that holds that when a contractor follows the plans and specifications furnished by the owner, and those plans and specifications turn out to be defective or insufficient, the contractor is not liable to the owner for any loss or damage resulting from the defective plans and specifications. The Spearin Doctrine's roots and name come from a 1918 United States Supreme Court decision, United States v. Spearin, 248 U.S. 132 (1918), which held that a contractor will not be liable to an owner for loss or damage that results solely from defects in the plan, design, or specifications provided to the contractor. The courts in virtually all states have adopted this rule.

Subcontractor is an individual or business that signs a contract to perform part or all of the obligations of a general contractor.

Surveys are a method of gathering information from individuals. Surveys may be conducted to gather information through a printed questionnaire, over the telephone, by mail, in person, or on the web. This information is collected through use of standardized procedures so that every participant is asked the same questions in the same way. It involves asking people for information in some structured format. Depending on what is being analyzed, the participants being surveyed may be representing themselves, their employer, or some organization to which they belong.

SWOT (strengths, weaknesses, opportunities and threats) is a common business analysis and marketing tool. It involves specifying the objective of the business venture or project and identifying the internal and external factors that are favorable and unfavorable to achieve that objective. Marketing managers using a SWOT analysis may list columns on a sheet a paper for each category, with intersecting rows for the marketing manager's company and relevant competitors. This creates a chart showing how the companies match up. Users of SWOT analysis need to ask and answer questions that generate meaningful information for each category to make the analysis useful and find their competitive advantage. SWOT is important because ithey can inform later steps in planning to achieve the objective.

Target audience is a specific group of people within the target market at which a product or the marketing message of a product is aimed at.

Tertiary target audience is the group of consumer who want to wait and see. They will wait for the product to be popular, the price within their purchasing range and if the product will answer their need at one point in time.

VoIP (Voice over IP) is a methodology and group of technologies for the delivery of voice communications and multimedia sessions over Internet Protocol (IP) networks, such as the Internet. Other terms commonly associated with VoIP are IP telephony, Internet telephony, broadband telephony, and broadband phone service. ■

ANNOTATED BIBLIOGRAPHY

Advertising Age. http://adage.com. An excellent resource for trends in advertising and marketing; of particular interest is the section on B-to-B marketing. Accessed January 5, 2015. http://bit.ly/btob-adage.

AECbytes. Accessed January 15, 2015. http://aecbytes.com. *AECbytes* is an online publication launched by Dr. Lachmi Khemlani in 2003. It focuses on researching, analyzing, and reviewing technology products and services for the building industry, as well as reviews on A/E/C technology.

American Institute of Architects and AIA California Council. Integrated Project Delivery: A Guide. (Sacramento, CA: AIA National & AIA California Council, 2007). Accessed January 5, 2015. http://bit.ly/aia-report. Originating at the regional level, this guide provides a systematic approach to team integration for alternative project delivery, specifically IPD and design-build.

ArchiCAD. 2012. "What is BIM?" Accessed January 5, 2015. http://bit.ly/bim-video. A short video explaining in simple terms what Building Information Modeling (BIM) is and how the industry is using it.

Baréz-Brown, Chris. *How to Have Kick-Ass Ideas: Shake Up Your Business, Shake Up Your Life* Paperback. (New York: Skyhorse Publishing, 2008). A fun book that will help you expand the range of your imagination, at work and at home.

Brogan, Chris and Julien Smith. *Trust Agents: Using the Web to Build Influence, Improve Reputation, and Earn Trust.* (Hoboken, NJ: John Wiley & Sons, Inc., 2009). How to use social networks and personal connections to drive marketing.

Capelin, Joan. *Communications by Design: Marketing Professional Services.* (Atlanta: Greenway Comm., 2004). Practical lessons for getting your message out and choosing your clients.

Collins, Jim. *Good to Great.* (New York: Collins, 2001). Forceful case studies that show how to turn competence into excellence.

Construction Management Association of America. *An Owner's Guide to Project Delivery Methods.* (McLean, VA: Construction Management Association of America, 2012). Accessed January 5, 2015. http://bit.ly/cmaa-guide. This guide provides fundamental concepts for considering APD, including differentiating various project delivery methods.

Crandall, Rick. *Marketing Your Services: For People Who Hate to Sell, 2nd ed. (New York: McGraw-Hill, 2002). A guide for business people about how to build relation*ships with customers to achieve success.

Dietz, Andrew. *The Opening Playbook: A Professional's Guide to Building Relationships that Grow Revenue.* (New York: McGraw-Hill Education, 2014). Focuses on the "opening plays" of a marketing strategy rather than the "closer" aspects that often get more attention.

Drucker, Peter F. *The Effective Executive: The Definitive Guide to Getting the Right Things Done,* (Harperbusiness Essentials), rev. ed. (New York: HarperBusiness, 2006). Although Drucker wrote this book more than 30 years ago, the principles of decision-making are still relevant today, and remains an invaluable resource.

Drucker, Peter F. *The Essential Drucker: The Best of Sixty Years of Peter Drucker's Essential Writings on Management* (Collins Business Essentials), rev. ed. (New York: HarperBusiness, 2008). An excellent compilation written over six decades, published in journals, magazines and over 30 books. Essential to anyone serious about the "management of an enterprise (and) the self-management of the individual, whether executive or professional, within an enterprise and altogether in our society of managed organizations."

Ferrazzi, Keith. *Never Eat Alone (And Other Secrets to Success, One Relationship at a Time).* (New York: Currency, Doubleday, 2005). A fun, easy read about developing better networking and stronger relationships.

Fulghum, Robert. *All I Really Need to Know I Learned in Kindergarten,* 15th ed. (New York: Ballantine Books, 2004). A collection of short essays that are ruminations on topics ranging from holidays, childhood and death, that offers uncommon insight on everyday occurrences.

Gerwick, Jr., Ben C. *Construction of Marine and Offshore Structures*, 3rd ed. (United Kingdom: Taylor & Francis Group: CRC Press, 2007). Captures the current state of practice and presents it in a straightforward, easy digestible manner that has made this volume the reference of choice for modern civic and maritime construction engineers.

Godin, Seth. *Permission Marketing: Turning Strangers into Friends, and Friends into Customers,* 1st ed. (New York: Simon & Schuster, 1999). Shows how to build an ongoing relationship of increasing depth with customers; the opposite of "interruption marketing."

Goleman, Daniel, Richard Boyatzis, and Annie McKee. *Primal Leadership: Realizing the Power of Emotional Intelligence.* (Boston, MA: Harvard Business School Press, 2002). A great primer on emotional intelligence and effective leadership.

Harding, Ford. *Rain Making: Attract New Clients No Matter What Your Field,* 2nd ed. (Avon, MA: Adams Business, 2008). A classic on business development in the professional services industry with many practical, easy-to-learn, and easy-to-use techniques.

High Performance Outcomes. Accessed January 5, 2015. http://www.highperformanceoutcomes. blogspot.com. Contemporary articles by David Shelton for IPD, design-build, CM@Risk, and other alternative project delivery methods, 2011-2014. With commentary written from the project owner's perspective, these articles break down APD by considering the mechanics of project delivery, common misconceptions, and a critique of traditional mindsets from the owner, designer, and builder.

Jacques, Richard G. *It's About Them: Building the Market-Driven Organization.* (Canton, CT: Jacques Management LLC, 2010). Many personal case studies that nicely demonstrate the importance of knowing the clients' needs better than they do.

Jones, Stephen A. *SmartMarket Report: The Business Value of BIM for Construction in Global Markets,* (New York: McGraw Hill Construction, 2014). Accessed January 5, 2015. http://bit.ly/ smartmarket-report. Research on implementation, ROI, business benefits, and planned investments in BIM by contractors in 10 global regions.

Jones, Stephen A. *The Business Value of BIM in North America.* (New York: McGraw Hill Construction, 2013). Accessed January 5, 2015. http://bit.ly/ViClzO. Research on adoption, implementation, ROI, business benefits, and planned investments in BIM by owners, contractors, architects, and engineers in North America, including case studies on successful BIM usage.

Kim, W. Chan and Renée Mauborgne. *Blue Ocean Strategy: How to Create Uncontested Market Space and Make the Competition Irrelevant,* 2nd ed. (Boston, MA: Harvard Business School Press, 2005). Argues that leading companies will succeed not by battling competitors, but by creating "blue oceans" of uncontested market space that are primed for growth.

Klabunde, Tim. *Network Like an Introvert: A New Way of Thinking about Business Relationships.* (Nepean, ON Canada: Asset Beam Publishing, Ltd., 2012). A quick read that may change the way you think about networking.

Kumar, Nirmalya. *Marketing as Strategy.* (Boston, MA: Harvard Business School Press, 2004). Outlines organization-wide transformational initiatives that win marketing a prominent seat at the executive table.

Levitt, Theodore M. *Marketing Imagination,* expanded ed. (New York: Free Press, 1986). This classic book first published in 1986 offers rich insight in the marketing world.

Lowe, Suzanne. *The Integration Imperative: Erasing Marketing and Business Development Silos – Once and for All – in Professional Service Firms.* (Concord, MA: Professional Services Books, 2009). Discusses how best to integrate marketing and business development functions.

MarketingSherpa. Accessed January 5, 2015. http://www.marketingsherpa.com/. MarketingSherpa is a research institute specializing in tracking what works in all aspects of marketing. Provides practical case studies, research, and training for marketers; you can subscribe to regular emails.

McDonald, Kelly. *How to Market to People Not Like You.* (Hoboken, NJ: John Wiley & Sons, Inc., 2011). Understanding your clients of today and tomorrow, particularly if they are different from you.

McGraw-Hill Construction. *SmartMarket Report: Information Mobility: Improving Team Collaboration through the Movement of Project Information, 2013.* Accessed January 5, 2015. http://bit.ly/smartmarket-2013. This 48-page report looks at how project information flows between project partners, between the office and the jobsite and between systems within a company. It examines the degree to which information mobility has enhanced productivity and collaboration for contractors, and it demonstrates the gaps that must be addressed to help the industry to continue to improve.

McKain, Scott. *Collapse of Distinction: Stand Out and Move Up While Your Competition Fails.* (Nashville, TN: Thomas Nelson, 2009). When companies are perceived as the same, customers will choose based on price. This book educates readers on the importance of distinction and how they can create it for their companies.

Messner, John. *The BIM Project Execution Planning Guide V2.0.* (Penn State Univ. Computer Integrated Construction (CIC) Research Program, 2013). Accessed January 5, 2015. http://bim.psu.edu/. Templated guide to establish objectives and assign responsibilities for the use of BIM on a specific project.

Miles, Josh. *Bold Brand.* (Cleveland, OH: Content Marketing Institute, LLC, 2012). A fun-to-read, comprehensive guide that covers how professional services firms can establish and grow bold brands.

Miller, Jack. *Jack Miller Network.* Accessed January 5, 2015. http://www.jackmiller.com. A newsworthy blog run by a civil engineer and successful investor.

Miller, Kevin T., Ronald D. Worth, and Michael T. Kubal. *A/E/C Marketing Fundamentals.* (Vista, CA: BNI Publications, Inc., 2005). This first edition of this volume provides marketers with the resources and ideas to adopt to the numerous standard changes in the A/E/C industry.

Quatman, G. William and Ranjit Dhar. *The Architect's Guide to Design–Build Services,* 1st ed. (Hoboken, NJ: John Wiley & Sons Inc., 2003). From the professional architect's perspective, this guide provides commentary on how practice changes when delivering design-build, specifically with respect to roles, responsibilities, and legal impacts.

Richter, Sam. *Take the Cold Out of Cold Calling: Web Search Secrets,* 5th ed. (Edina, MN: Adams Business & Professional, 2010). How to find better information online about potential clients and effectively eliminate "cold" calls.

Richter, Sam. *Warm Call Center.* Accessed January 5, 2015. http://www.warmcallcenter.com. This newsletter is a powerful resource that provides numerous tips on using the web to access the information you need to understand your prospective clients, and to beat your competition.

Sanvido, Victor and Mark Konchar. "Project Delivery Systems: CM at Risk, Design-Build, Design-Bid-Build." *Construction Industry Institute Research Report,* 133–11. (Austin, TX: Construction

Industry Institute, 1998). Accessed January 5, 2015. http://bit.ly/ciir-report. Research comparing design-build, design-bid-build, and construction management at risk project delivery systems.

Schultz, Don and Heidi Schultz. *IMC: The Next Generation.* (New York: McGraw-Hill, 2004). Tackles the importance of integrating internal and external communication into a dynamic, value-adding asset.

Society for Marketing Professional Services and SMPS Foundation. *Marketing Handbook for the Design & Construction Professional,* 3rd ed. (Los Angeles: BNi Building News, 2009). Explores many of the issues introduced in A/E/C Marketing Fundamentals in great detail.

SMPS Foundation. *A/E/C BUSINESS DEVELOPMENT: The Decade Ahead.* (Thought Leadership Series Committee) (Charleston, SC: SMPS Foundation, 2013). Buyers and sellers of professional services outline their preferences and insights on effective business development strategies and trends.

Society for Marketing Professional Services. www.smps.org. Accessed January 5, 2015. Past SMPS Marketing Communication Award winners; selected clarification statements available by contacting the Society for Marketing Professional Services. A great resource to find inspiration through award-winning marketing tactics and tools used by firms in the A/E/C industry.

The Wall Street Journal. http://online.wsj.com. Always an excellent source of news that affects your customers. Of particular interest is the regular section, "Media Marketing." Accessed January 5, 2015. http://online.wsj.com/public/page/news-media-marketing.html.

Turminello, Randy. *What You Need to Know about Doughnuts — And 35 More Marketing Success Stories.* (Alexandria, VA: SMPS, 2003). Covers principles, strategies and real life examples to ensure your marketing efforts are not wasted. Includes interesting statistics, quick summaries, and important rules of thumb for professional service marketers. ■

ABOUT THE PHOTOGRAPHERS

PAUL TURANG is an award-winning photographer who has been photographing architecture and design-related projects for nearly 20 years. Based in Los Angeles, Turang and his team have photographed projects throughout the nation. His images have received several international photography awards and have been featured in a variety of design related publications including *Architectural Record; Buildings: Healthcare Design, Hospitality and Design; Interiors and Sources; Metropolis; LD+A;* and others. Turang travels regularly for assignments bringing his passion and vision to leading architecture, design, and construction firms. Turang is a member of several trade organizations, including the American Society of Media Photographers (ASMP), Society for Marketing Professional Service (SMPS) and AIA Affiliate. His website is http://paulturang.com and he can be contacted at paul@paulturang.com. ■

SAM KITTNER is a marketing and corporate communications photographer based in Washington, DC. Kittner's architectural, portrait, and scene-setting photographs appear in publications world-wide. He is commissioned regularly by media, institutional, and corporate clients to photograph their people and projects throughout the globe for a wide range of collateral. Kittner's work has been recognized by the leading graphics trade publications *Communication Arts* and *Photo District News.* Kittner's images document and promote the exciting urban renaissance our nation is experiencing. With a photojournalism background including assignments for publications such as *Time, People,* and *Business Week,* Kittner tells his clients' stories through engaging and dynamic photographs. He also produces documentary and fine arts prints, which have been displayed widely at venues including Corcoran Gallery of Art and Smithsonian National Museum of Natural History. Kittner studied economics at the University of North Carolina, and is a member of Society for Marketing Professional Service (SMPS) Washington DC and the American Society of Media Photographers (ASMP). His website is http://kittner.com and he can be contacted at sam@kittner.com. ■

PHOTO CREDITS

Cover:

RADY School of Management at UC San Diego. Copyright © 2008 by Paul Turang.

Chapter Headings:

Introduction (p. 1):   "Jacobs Medical Center." Copyright © 2014 by Paul Turang.

Chapter 1 (p. 9):   "Constitution Avenue" (Washington, DC). Copyright © 2015 by Sam Kittner.

Chapter 2 (p. 25):   "Untitled." Copyright © 2015 by Sam Kittner.

Chapter 3 (p. 43):   "Construction of the Newseum" (Washington, DC). Copyright © 2015 by Sam Kittner.

Chapter 4 (p. 61):   "Pauley Pavilion at UCLA." Copyright © 2013 by Paul Turang.

Chapter 5 (p. 77):   "Concrete mat pour at the Montage Beverly Hills." Copyright © 2008 by Paul Turang.

Chapter 6 (p. 97):   "Construction of CityCenterDC" (Washington, DC). Copyright © 2015 by Sam Kittner.

Chapter 7 (p. 117):   "300 New Jersey Avenue" (Washington, DC). Copyright © 2015 by Sam Kittner.

Back Cover:

Image No. 1:   "Reston, VA." Copyright © 2015 by Sam Kittner.

Image No. 2:   "Trompe-l'oeil mural by Byron Peck/City Arts on the side of Kittner Studio building" (Takoma Park, MD). Copyright © 2015 by Sam Kittner.

Image No. 3:   "Constitution Avenue" (Washington, DC). Copyright © 2015 by Sam Kittner.

Image No. 4:   "Young Research Library at UCLA." Copyright © 2013 by Paul Turang.

Image No. 5:   "Blair Middle School." Copyright © 2012 by Paul Turang.

ABOUT THE AUTHORS

RICHARD A. BELLE, IOM, CAE, is President of Belle Communications, LLC, a communications consulting firm in Bethesda, MD, offering services in proposal coaching, technical writing, technical editing, communications audits, and awards coaching. Before establishing his consultancy, he held senior communications positions at the American Council of Engineering Companies, Design-Build Institute of America, and the Civil Engineering Research Foundation. Belle is the lead author of six industry monographs and dozens of articles, ranging from A/E/C benchmarking standards to safety opportunities using design-build. Belle served as editor of this second edition of *A/E/C Marketing Fundamentals* and was responsible for the updated focus, overall content, and recruitment of authors. ∎

HOLLY R. BOLTON, FSMPS, CPSM, has worn several hats during her 15-plus years of experience, including serving as Director of Marketing for CE Solutions, a structural engineering firm in Carmel, IN, providing marketing communications consulting to outside clients, marketing for a transportation engineering firm in Kansas City, directing communications for a multi-discipline design firm in Indianapolis, and fulfilling several roles at a small newspaper. Active in the Society for Marketing Professional Services at the chapter, regional, and national level, Bolton has served on the SMPS Board of Directors as chapter delegate and on the SMPS Foundation Board of Trustees. She has a BS in public relations and a creative writing minor from the University of Central Missouri. ∎

JULIE HUVAL, CPSM, joined Beck Technology to oversee the marketing and communications efforts of the software development and Building Information Modeling (BIM) consulting company. She has been an integral part of expanding the company's brand and is a resource to its long-term strategic planning. Through Beck Technology, Huval has developed relationships with leading industry futurists, which led her to host the webinar series, "Innovation in the AEC Industry." A former President of SMPS Dallas, Huval was inducted into the SMPS Dallas Marketing Hall of Fame in 2014. She earned an MBA from The University of Texas at Arlington, a BA in journalism and environmental studies from Baylor University, and is a Certified Professional Services Marketer. ∎

STEPHEN A. JONES, Senior Director at McGraw Hill Construction, focuses on how emerging economic and technology trends are transforming the construction industry. In addition to hundreds of global speaking engagements and numerous articles in industry publications, he authors many of McGraw-Hill's *SmartMarket Reports* on key industry trends, which are read by millions worldwide and frequently cited as authoritative references. Jones also hosts the ENR FutureTech and High Performance Construction events that address how advanced technologies, streamlined workflows, emerging performance metrics, and new business models are shaping the future of our industry. Before joining McGraw-Hill, Jones held senior creative and management positions at Primavera Systems (now part of Oracle) and at a number of top design firms, most recently with Burt Hill (now merged with Stantec). He holds an MBA from the Wharton School of the University of Pennsylvania, and a BA from The Johns Hopkins University. ∎

KEVIN MILLER is the founder and President of Frost Miller Group, a marketing communication firm headquartered in the Washington, DC area. Founded in 1992, Frost Miller works with businesses and organizations across the U.S and abroad, including dozens of companies in the commercial real estate industry. Frost Miller provides strategic planning, web development, graphic design, PR, and social media support. Prior to forming Frost Miller, Miller spent five years as the Director of Marketing Communication for Clark Construction. He has co-authored two books on marketing communication, as well as numerous blogs and articles, and speaks regularly about marketing communication issues and trends. ∎

DAVID M. SHELTON, 3PQC, DBIA, AIA, is a prominent innovator, developer, and practitioner within the design and construction industry for strategic project planning and acquisition. As a co-founder of DesignSense (founded in 1999), he has developed and achieved major industry advances in the structure and convention of project planning, delivery, and document systems for many forms of alternative project delivery, including construction management, design-build, and integrated project delivery. As author of the *3PQ Acquisition & Management Systems,* Shelton has facilitated project owner groups and developed the most advanced performance-based acquisition documents for a variety of project types. He also provides professional training on integrated delivery methods in a variety of venues and was a co-founder and charter member of the Design-Build Institute of America Mid-America Chapter. ■

RONALD D. WORTH was chief executive officer of the Society for Marketing Professional Services (SMPS) (1999-2015), a network of 6,300 marketing and business development professionals working in architectural, engineering, planning, interior design, construction, and specialty construction firms located throughout the United States and Canada. Worth also served as the Executive Director of the Professional Services Management Association, representing CEOs and CFOs of leading architectural and engineering companies, and the Washington Building Congress. He has conducted more than 300 seminars and training classes for approximately 14,000 professionals across the country on topics from marketing, building industry economics, technology in construction, and preconstruction services, to economical structural design of various building types. ■

INDEX

R

Rain Making: Attracting New Clients No Matter What Your Field, 64
request for proposal (RFP), 16, 21, 22, 53, 54, 63, 64, 119, 127, 132, 133
request for qualifications (RFQ), 52, 64, 119, 132, 133, 135
résumés, 133, 135
Richter, Sam, 74
Robertson, Kim 122
Rose, Robert, 80

S

sales, 3, 12, 16-18, 70, 74, 81-84, 94, 99, 110, 113, 120, 131
search engines, 75
seminars, 74, 129
Sides, Richard, 82
situational analysis, 83
SmithGroupJJR, 131, 141
SMPS (Society for Marketing Professional Service), 3-5, 81, 124, 128, 133
social media, 4, 82, 120, 122, 123, 127, 130, 131, 136
Spearin Doctrine, 52
strategies, 4, 5, 10, 12-15, 23, 45, 66, 75, 85, 92, 119-121
Strategies That Work, 82
surveys, 68, 88, 132
SWOT, 62, 67, 68, 84, 87, 89

T

Take the Cold Out of Cold Calling: Web Search Secret, 74
target audience, 98-101, 105, 107-111, 113, 120-126, 129, 132
team, 28-32, 36-38, 82-86, 91-93, 106, 110, 112, 114, 125-128, 133-135
technology, 4, 5, 12, 15, 27-40, 46, 87, 120, 122, 136
three-dimensional (3D), 13, 29, 32, 36
trade publications, 122, 161
trade shows, 11, 126
training, 63, 87, 90, 129
Tuminello, Randy, 81
Twitter, 65, 127, 130
two-dimensional (2D), 29, 32

V

video, 12, 29, 35, 130, 131, 136
virtual, 10-12, 17, 22, 23, 27, 29-32, 34, 36

Society for Marketing Professional Services

THE SOCIETY FOR MARKETING PROFESSIONAL SERVICES (SMPS) is a community of marketing and business development professionals working to secure profitable business relationships for their A/E/C companies. Through networking, business intelligence, and research, SMPS members gain a competitive advantage in positioning their firms successfully in the marketplace. SMPS offers members professional development, leadership opportunities, and marketing resources to advance their careers.

SMPS is the only organization dedicated to creating business opportunities in the A/E/C industry. Companies tap into a powerful national and regional network to form teams, secure business referrals and intelligence, and benchmark performance. SMPS was created in 1973 by a small group of professional services firm leaders who recognized the need to sharpen skills, pool resources, and work together to build their businesses.

Today, SMPS represents a dynamic network of approximately 6,000 marketing and business development professionals from architectural, engineering, planning, interior design, construction, and specialty consulting firms located throughout the United States and Canada. The Society and its chapters benefit from the support of 3,700 design and building firms, encompassing 80 percent of the *Engineering News–Record* Top 500 Design Firms and Top 400 Contractors.

For more information, visit our website at:
www.smps.org

CPSIA information can be obtained
at www.ICGtesting.com
Printed in the USA
BVHW06s1521080418
512537BV00003B/3/P